Diagnostic
Assessment

Mc Graw Hill **Macmillan/McGraw-Hill Glencoe**

Acknowledgments

The publisher gratefully acknowledges permission to reprint the following copyrighted material:

Excerpts "Critchlow Verbal Language Scales" by Donald E. Critchlow are from Consortium On Reading Excellence (CORE): Assessing Reading Multiple Measures for Kindergarten Through Eighth Grade. Copyright © 1999 by Consortium On Reading Excellence (CORE). Reprinted by permission of Arena Press.

Excerpt "Metacomprehension Strategy Index" by Maribeth C. Schmitt includes information from 2007 Applestar Productions Web site: http://www.applestar.org/Recent/Metacognition_presentation.pdf by Jean Marrapodi, Ph.D.

Excerpts "Phonological Awareness Screening Test" by Marilyn Jager Adams, Ph.D., Barbara R. Foorman, Ph.D., Ingvar Lundberg, Ph.D., and Terri Beeler, Ed.D. are from Consortium On Reading Excellence (CORE): Assessing Reading Multiple Measures for Kindergarten Through Eighth Grade. Copyright © 1999 by Consortium On Reading Excellence (CORE). Reprinted by permission of Arena Press.

Excerpts "McLeod Assessment of Reading Comprehension" by John McLeod, Ph.D. and Rita McLeod, Ph.D. are from Consortium On Reading Excellence (CORE): Assessing Reading Multiple Measures for Kindergarten Through Eighth Grade. Copyright © 1999 by Consortium On Reading Excellence (CORE). Reprinted by permission of Arena Press.

Excerpts are from "Words Their Way: Word Study for Phonics, Vocabulary, and Spelling Instruction" by Donald Bear, Marcia Invernizzi, Shane Templeton, and Francine Johnston. Copyright © 2008 by Pearson Prentice Hall.

Excerpts "Words Their Way: Qualitative Spelling Inventory" by Donald Bear, Marcia Invernizzi, Shane Templeton, and Francine Johnston are from Consortium On Reading Excellence (CORE): Assessing Reading Multiple Measures for Kindergarten Through Eighth Grade. Copyright © 1999 by Consortium On Reading Excellence (CORE). Reprinted by permission of Arena Press.

Excerpts from "Scaffolded Writing Instruction: Teaching With a Gradual-Release Framework" are by Douglas Fisher and Nancy Frey. Copyright © 2007 by Douglas Fisher and Nancy Frey. Printed with permission.

Excerpt: "CORE Phoneme Deletion Test" by Orna Lenchner, Ph.D. from Consortium On Reading Excellence (CORE): Assessing Reading Multiple Measures for Kindergarten Through Eighth Grade. Copyright © 1999 by Consortium On Reading Excellence (CORE). Reprinted by permission of Arena Press.

A

The McGraw·Hill Companies

 Macmillan/McGraw-Hill

Contents

Informal Reading Inventory for Grades 1–6

Spelling for Grades K–6

Vocabulary for Grades K–6

Reading Comprehension for Grades K–6

Introduction

Overview

The purpose of this *Diagnostic Assessment* book is to provide you with assessment options to measure critical components of reading across grades K–6. This book includes a large portion of the assessments recommended for use with *Treasures*. Its primary focus is on assessments that can be used for **screening** and **placement** into an instructional level of *Treasures*: on grade level, beyond level, approaching level, or needs intervention. This book is designed to help you manage the use of multiple assessments, compare and interpret the results, and then use that information for instructional planning. It provides basic definitions and clear guidance on how test scores can be a useful resource for addressing your students' needs.

Separate, self-contained assessment components, including the *Student's Weekly Assessment, Unit Assessment, Benchmark Assessment, Fluency Assessment,* and *Running Records* books, also are provided as a part of the *Treasures* materials.

What is assessment?

- Assessment is the process of systematically gathering evidence about what students know and can do.

- Assessments can be both formal and informal as long as the information is systematically collected, scored, and recorded.

Types of assessment

There are many different types of assessment. Usually, an assessment is designed with one specific purpose in mind, and using the test for that purpose gives the most accurate (valid and reliable) scores. In practice, however, many tests are used for more than one purpose. For example, some teachers may use a norm-referenced standardized test both for determining how much a student has learned *and* for diagnosing what the student needs to learn in the future. Although using one particular test for more than one purpose is not necessarily wrong, the results for the secondary purpose need to be interpreted with caution, and the use of multiple sources of information becomes critical.

Screening and **Diagnostic Assessments** often are used together and complement each other. A **screening** test is a short, skill-specific instrument that can be administered quickly to give a general idea of what a student knows. Screening tests are good for telling teachers one of two alternatives: "The student knows it" *or* "The student doesn't know it." Cut scores that identify these alternatives usually are conservative, or high, which will result in more of the "doesn't know it" students than may actually be the case. The

Introduction

consequence of not meeting the cut score of a screening test is taking the diagnostic test. The underlying premise of the conservative decision is that we don't want to set the expectations for a student higher than his or her skill level can handle in the classroom. Taking the time, early, to do a more thorough skill analysis using a diagnostic assessment is much better than trying to go back and pick up the missing pieces behind a failing child.

A **diagnostic** assessment is an expanded screening test that provides more items and additional ways to determine a student's knowledge of a skill and to monitor the student's progress with that skill throughout the school year. The greater number of items creates a more reliable test, which can make you more confident about decision-making for instructional purposes. A diagnostic test can be administered individually or in a group, depending on the original design of the test. The results of the test can be used to determine a starting point for instruction and for assigning small skill-based groups for extra attention. Diagnostic tests are best administered after the cut score *is not made* on a related screening test and at the beginning of the school year or when a new student enters the class. Occasionally, teachers decide to administer a diagnostic test to everyone in a classroom, skipping the screening test entirely. Although this practice is not wrong, it may result in unnecessary testing of students who already have solid, grade-level or above reading skills.

A **placement** test is a type of diagnostic test. Placement tests are group administered and help you decide on an appropriate instructional level for the student. However, a placement test alone may not provide specific, detailed information about the strengths and weaknesses of a student's skills. Instead, you should use the skill-specific tests included in this book, such as the Phonological Awareness Screening Test or Informal Reading Inventory, to help you make decisions about placing students in the *Treasures* program.

Introduction

Progress monitoring assessments are used to keep tabs on the growth or maintenance of a student's skills. These tests can be categorized as **formative** assessments because they are given more than once, over time, and rarely have high stakes attached. The primary purpose of a progress monitoring or any other formative assessment is to allow you to make immediate, corrective instructional decisions. Formative test results allow you to try alternative teaching methods during the school year, before the administration of a high-stakes test, such as a state test used for accountability purposes.

State tests with high-stakes decisions attached are called **summative,** or **outcome,** assessments. A summative assessment gives a judgment about whether the tested material has been learned. The consequences of summative assessments can be harsh. A student with low test scores may have to repeat a grade or attend summer school. For a teacher or a principal, low summative test results can mean school closings or lost jobs. Therefore, the assessments usually are made with great care and are tested and reviewed by hundreds or thousands of people before they are administered. The scores on these tests generally provide an accurate understanding of a student's general skill level. They cover the broad domain of a particular concept to give an overall perception of learning. Most often, they are not designed for diagnosing a student's specific skill weaknesses, but they can paint a picture of general strong and weak spots when a class, a school, or a district's scores are examined. Sometimes teachers use the results of a summative assessment for diagnosing a student's particular skill strengths, especially when no other test scores are available to guide decision making. Although it is not wrong to use these scores for this purpose, there may not be enough items per standard, or not all standards may be included, to make accurate instructional decisions. Using multiple sources of information, including teacher judgment and other available test results, is critical for making these decisions useful.

Introduction

Using Multiple Measures
The Assessment Process

The assessment process is about making instructional decisions based on assessment information. To the greatest extent possible, all instructional decisions should be based on **multiple sources** of valid and reliable information.

- The process starts with measurement and scoring (test results, observations).

- The next step is to compare and interpret the information you have gathered.

- The third step is to make instructional decisions based on your conclusions.

- This process is ongoing: measure, interpret, make decisions. . . .

The Assessment Process

Measure and Score
Use multiple sources of evidence (test scores, observations).

Interpret
Compare and contrast scores and observations with other assessment results.

Make Instructional Decisions
based on your findings.

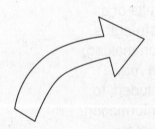

Diagnostic Assessment

Introduction

Placement Assessments

Using Assessment to Place Students into the Treasures Program

The **Diagnostic Assessment** book offers assessments to help you make decisions about where to place students in the *Treasures* program. Based on the assessment results, guidelines are offered to place students in

- On Grade Level Materials

- Approaching Grade Level Materials

- Beyond Grade Level Materials

- Intervention

The ultimate goal for classroom assessments in making placement decisions is to minimize the amount of testing needed to get the most valid and reliable information so that you can provide the most suitable level of learning for each student. Using an appropriate type of test, with the best order of delivery, will help you reach this goal. Careful planning of your testing needs can help to eliminate the confusion and lost time caused by jumping from test to test to individually match ever-changing student needs. The charts that follow are designed as a guide to support your *Treasures* placement testing plan. They provide recommendation of tests and cut scores for decision making.

Placement Decisions for Grade K

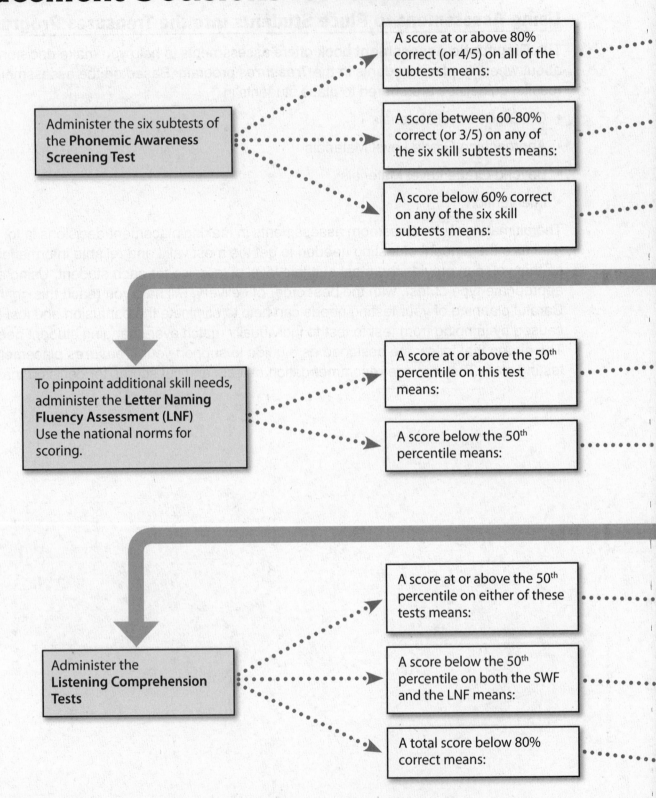

Administer the six subtests of the **Phonemic Awareness Screening Test**

A score at or above 80% correct (or 4/5) on all of the subtests means:

A score between 60-80% correct (or 3/5) on any of the six skill subtests means:

A score below 60% correct on any of the six skill subtests means:

To pinpoint additional skill needs, administer the **Letter Naming Fluency Assessment (LNF)** Use the national norms for scoring.

A score at or above the 50th percentile on this test means:

A score below the 50th percentile means:

Administer the **Listening Comprehension Tests**

A score at or above the 50th percentile on either of these tests means:

A score below the 50th percentile on both the SWF and the LNF means:

A total score below 80% correct means:

Diagnostic Assessment

Introduction

The student should be placed in the *Treasures* **On Level** materials.

The student can be placed in the *Treasures* **Approaching Level** materials and should participate in small, flexible, skill-based groups based on the assessment results.

The student can be placed in the *Treasures* **Approaching Level** materials or you can consider the *Reading Triumphs* **Intervention Program** for more intensive instruction.

The student should be placed in the *Treasures* **Approaching Level** materials and should participate in small group, skill-based instruction based on the results of the Phonemic Awareness Screening Test.

The student can be placed in the *Treasures* **Approaching Level** materials or you can consider the *Reading Triumphs* **Intervention Program** for more intensive instruction.

STOP PLACEMENT TESTING.

The student should be placed in the *Treasures* **Beyond Level** materials.

STOP PLACEMENT TESTING.

The student is ready for the *Treasures* **On Level materials**.

The student should be placed in the *Treasures* **Approaching Level** materials and should have **additional testing** to pinpoint specific skill challenges.

Placement Decisions for Grades 1 - 2

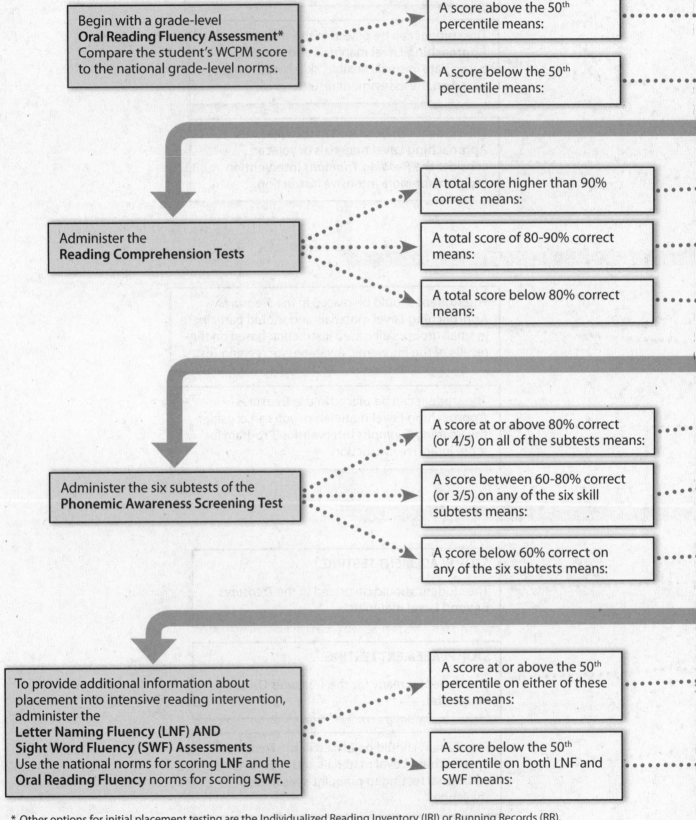

Begin with a grade-level **Oral Reading Fluency Assessment*** Compare the student's WCPM score to the national grade-level norms.

- A score above the 50th percentile means:
- A score below the 50th percentile means:

Administer the **Reading Comprehension Tests**

- A total score higher than 90% correct means:
- A total score of 80-90% correct means:
- A total score below 80% correct means:

Administer the six subtests of the **Phonemic Awareness Screening Test**

- A score at or above 80% correct (or 4/5) on all of the subtests means:
- A score between 60-80% correct (or 3/5) on any of the six skill subtests means:
- A score below 60% correct on any of the six subtests means:

To provide additional information about placement into intensive reading intervention, administer the **Letter Naming Fluency (LNF) AND Sight Word Fluency (SWF) Assessments** Use the national norms for scoring **LNF** and the **Oral Reading Fluency** norms for scoring **SWF.**

- A score at or above the 50th percentile on either of these tests means:
- A score below the 50th percentile on both LNF and SWF means:

* Other options for initial placement testing are the Individualized Reading Inventory (IRI) or Running Records (RR).

Diagnostic Assessment

Introduction

STOP PLACEMENT TESTING.
The student should be placed in the *Treasures* **On Level** materials.

Administer additional assessments to determine underlying skill strengths and weaknesses.

STOP PLACEMENT TESTING.
The student should be placed in the *Treasures* **Beyond Level** materials.

STOP PLACEMENT TESTING.
The student should be placed in the *Treasures* **On Level** materials.

The student should be placed in the *Treasures* **Approaching Level** materials and have additional testing to pinpoint specific skill challenges.

The student should be placed in the *Treasures* **On Level** materials.

The student can be placed in the *Treasures* **Approaching Level** materials and should participate in small, flexible, skill-based groups based on the assessment results.

The student should be placed in the *Treasures* **Approaching Level** materials and should participate in small, flexible, skill-based groups based on the assessment results.
The student should be considered for more intensive reading intervention in the *Reading Triumphs* **Intervention Program.**

Intensive intervention most likely is NOT needed.
The student should be placed in the *Treasures* **Approaching Level** materials and should participate in small, flexible, skill-based groups.

The student needs to receive intensive reading instruction as soon as possible.
Once these skills are mastered, the student can transition out of intensive instruction and continue to work in small, flexible, skill-based groups and in the *Treasures* **Approaching Level** materials.

Placement Decisions for Grades 3 - 6

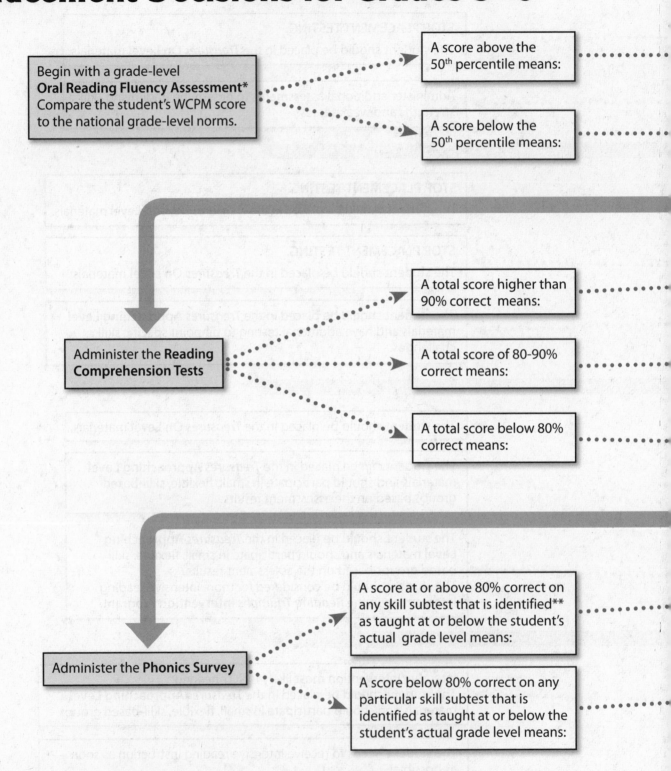

Begin with a grade-level **Oral Reading Fluency Assessment*** Compare the student's WCPM score to the national grade-level norms.

A score above the 50th percentile means:

A score below the 50th percentile means:

Administer the **Reading Comprehension Tests**

A total score higher than 90% correct means:

A total score of 80-90% correct means:

A total score below 80% correct means:

Administer the **Phonics Survey**

A score at or above 80% correct on any skill subtest that is identified** as taught at or below the student's actual grade level means:

A score below 80% correct on any particular skill subtest that is identified as taught at or below the student's actual grade level means:

* Other options for initial placement testing are the Individualized Reading Inventory (IRI) or Running Records (RR).
** Refer to the Phonics Survey scoring sheet on pages 83-84 for identification of skills usually taught at certain grade levels.

Introduction

STOP PLACEMENT TESTING.
The student should be placed in the *Treasures* On Level materials.

Administer additional assessments to determine underlying skill strengths and weaknesses.

STOP PLACEMENT TESTING.
The student should be placed in the *Treasures* **Beyond Level** materials.

STOP PLACEMENT TESTING.
The student should be placed in the *Treasures* On Level materials.

The student should be placed in the *Treasures* **Approaching Level** materials and have additional testing to pinpoint specific skill challenges.

The student should be placed in the *Treasures* **Approaching Level** materials.

Use the lower subsection scores to organize small group skill-differentiated instruction. Overall, the student can be placed in the *Treasures* **Approaching Level** materials and participate in small, flexible, skill-based groups according to assessment results. The student should be considered for more intensive reading intervention using the *Reading Triumphs* **Intervention Program**.

Introduction

Assessment Planning and Pacing Guide

Beyond the initial placement of students into the appropriate *Treasures* level of materials, students need to be tested periodically to determine whether they are progressing on a grade-level or faster pace. Many teachers administer these progress monitoring or benchmark tests on a regular schedule throughout the year: fall, winter, and spring, or over a regular period of time, such as every four to six weeks. The chart that follows provides a general testing scheduling guide by type of test, grade level, and time of year. The chart is designed to help you develop a testing plan for the entire school year. A school-year plan does not need to include a large number of tests; the tests that are selected should be relevant to the learning needs of your students.

Diagnostic Assessment

Introduction

Reading Component	Assessment	Grade Level						
		K	1	2	3	4	5	6
Phonemic Awareness	Phonological Awareness Screening	Beginning, Middle, and End of Year			Only if needed			
	Distinguishing Initial, Medial, and Final Sounds	Beginning, Middle, and End of Year			Only if needed			
	Phoneme Segmentation Fluency	Beginning, Middle, and End of Year			Only if needed			
	Phoneme Deletion	Beginning, Middle, and End of Year			Only if needed			
	Phoneme Substitution	Beginning, Middle, and End of Year			Only if needed			
Letter Naming and Sight Words	Letter Naming Fluency	Beginning, Middle, and End of Year	Beginning and Middle of Year		Not Applicable			
	Sight Word Fluency	Middle and End of Year	Beginning, Middle, and End of Year		Not Applicable			
Phonics and Decoding	Phonics Survey	Beginning, Middle, and End of Year			Only if needed			
Fluency	Oral Reading Fluency	Not Applicable	Middle and End of Year		Beginning, Middle, and End of Year			
	Running Records*	Not Applicable	Middle and End of Year		Every Three to Four Weeks			
	Informal Reading Inventory	Not Applicable	Beginning, Middle, and End of Year					
Spelling	Qualitative Spelling Index	End of Year	Beginning, Middle, and End of Year					
Vocabulary	Critchlow Verbal Language Scales	Middle and End of Year	Beginning, Middle, and End of Year					
Comprehension	Comprehension Passages	Beginning of Year						
	Diagnostic Assessment of Reading Comprehension**	Not Applicable			Beginning of Year			
	McLeod Assessment of Reading Comprehension	Not Applicable			Beginning of Year			
	Metacomprehension Strategy Index	Not Applicable			Beginning of Year			
English Language Proficiency	Oral Language Proficiency Benchmark Assessment***	Not Applicable	Beginning of Year					

* See **Running Records** book.
** You can find DARC on the Center for Applied Linguistics Web site: **http://www.cal.org/projects/darc.html**.
*** See **ELL Resource Book.**

Introduction

Assessment Record Sheet

Student Name _____   Date/Time of Year _____

Reading Component	Assessments	Scores	Observations	Next Steps
Phonemic Awareness	Phonological Awareness Screening			
	Distinguishing Initial, Medial, and Final Sounds			
	Phoneme Segmentation Fluency			
	Phoneme Deletion			
	Phoneme Substitution			
Letter Naming and Sight Words	Letter Naming Fluency			
	Sight Word Fluency			
Phonics and Decoding	Phonics Survey			
Fluency	Oral Reading Fluency			
	Running Records*			
	Informal Reading Inventory			
Spelling	Qualitative Spelling Index			
Vocabulary	Critchlow Verbal Language Scales			
Comprehension	Comprehension Passages			
	Diagnostic Assessment of Reading Comprehension**			
	McLeod Assessment of Reading Comprehension			
	Metacomprehension Strategy Index			
English Language Proficiency	Oral Language Proficiency Benchmark Assessment***			

* See **Running Records** book.
** You can find DARC on the Center for Applied Linguistics Web site: **http://www.cal.org/projects/darc.html**.
*** See **ELL Resource Book.**

Introduction

Assessments in this Book

This book includes assessments in the following areas:

- **Phonemic Awareness** Students who struggle with decoding often lack the ability to perceive and manipulate sounds (phonemes) in spoken words. Phonemic Awareness strongly correlates to early reading growth and is a key skill to assess with beginning readers.

- **Phonics and Decoding** Basic decoding proficiency and mastery of sound-spelling relationships is necessary for reading success. Decoding proficiency can be assessed using lists of real and pseudowords.

- **Oral Reading Fluency** The hallmark of a skilled reader is one who can decode and comprehend simultaneously. Oral reading fluency assessments determine which students are above, on, or below level for reading grade-level text. Oral reading fluency assessments correlate strongly to standardized comprehension assessments and are a quick measure to determine students' overall reading proficiency. These assessments can also be used to monitor the effect of instructional modifications or interventions as they are very sensitive to reading growth.

- **Informal Reading Inventory** A skilled reader also reads silently and orally with comprehension and accuracy. This assessment measures independent, instructional, and frustrational reading levels and provides you with greater understanding of a student's strengths and weaknesses in word recognition, word meaning, reading strategies, and comprehension.

- **Spelling** Spelling ability supports fluent reading and writing. Students use their knowledge of spelling patterns when reading and writing.

- **Vocabulary** Vocabulary knowledge is also highly correlated to comprehension. The more words a student knows and the deeper that knowledge, the more likely he or she will be able to comprehend the text.

- **Reading Comprehension** The goal of reading is comprehension, or overall understanding of the text. Reading Comprehension assessments determine at which grade level students can successfully comprehend text. These assessments are useful for providing leveled practice materials and serve as a starting point for instruction as you move struggling students to grade-level proficiency.

Introduction

Screening Options

Screening Students K-3

Most states or school districts identify the screening assessment you should use with your students, such as DIBELS or TPRI. It is recommended that you use the approved screening assessment in your state to identify at-risk students. We provide the information needed to align both **DIBELS (pages 17–21)** and **TPRI (pages 22–24)** to **TREASURES** on the indicated pages.

DIBELS (Dynamic Indicators of Basic Early Literacy Skills), K–3

DIBELS are short, one-minute fluency measures. The probes are individually administered, and measure all of the following:

Reading First Component	DIBELS Measure	Grade Level
Phonemic Awareness	Initial Sound Fluency	K
	Phoneme Segmentation Fluency	K–1
Phonics	Nonsense Word Fluency	K–1
Fluency (Connected Text)	Oral Reading Fluency	1–3
Comprehension	Oral Reading and Retell Fluency	1–3
Vocabulary	Word Use Fluency	K–3

TPRI (Texas Primary Reading Inventory), K–3

The TPRI probes are individually administered, quick, and given at the beginning, middle, and end of the year. They measure all of the following:

Reading First Component	TPRI Measure	Grade Level
Phonemic Awareness	Blending: Onset—Rimes, Phonemes	K–1
Phonics	Graphophonemic Knowledge	K–1
	Word Reading	K–3
Fluency (Connected Text)	Reading Accuracy and Fluency	1–3
Comprehension	Listening/Reading Comprehension	K–1/1–3

Screening Students 4-6

For screening students in the upper grades, we have provided an **Oral Reading Fluency Assessment** on **pages 85–162**. Fiction and nonfiction passages are provided along with comprehension questions. The screening assessment should be administered three times a year to measure students' fluency in the fall, winter, and spring.

Diagnostic Assessment

Introduction

Using DIBELS for Screening

What is the DIBELS screening assessment?

- Dynamic Indicators of Basic Early Literacy Skills measures reading acquisition skills.

- DIBELS provides an indicator of how well children are likely to do in their overall reading performance by the end of the third grade.

- DIBELS identifies children who are at risk for reading difficulties before failure sets in, and determines appropriate instructional support.

What does it do?

- The DIBELS measures identify emerging literacy skills and risk status towards developing reading difficulties.

How does it work?

- Screening is administered to all students in the fall, mid-winter, and spring of each year, K–3.

- All measures are individually administered, and include scripted administration instructions.

- Each measure is timed for one minute, except for Initial Sounds Fluency.

- There are three or four short tasks at each grade level. Results help teachers identify skills, monitor progress, and intervene with students at risk.

What does it measure?

- **Letter Naming Fluency:** a student's knowledge of upper and lower-case letters arranged in a random order.

- **Initial Sound Fluency:** a student's ability to recognize and produce the initial sound in an orally presented word.

- **Phoneme Segmentation Fluency:** a student's ability to segment three and four phoneme words into their individual phonemes fluently.

- **Nonsense Word Fluency:** a student's knowledge of letter-sound correspondence and the student's ability to blend sounds into words.

- **Oral Reading and Retell Fluency:** a student's overall reading performance, and identifies students who may need additional instructional support in fluency and comprehension.

- **Word Use Fluency:** identifies students who may need additional instructional support with vocabulary strategies.

Aligning the DIBELS Screening Schedule with TREASURES
Kindergarten

TREASURES	DIBELS Measure	Start Smart/ Beginning	Unit 4/ Middle	Unit 9/ End
Phonemic Awareness	ISF	Goal: 8 Low Risk 8 or more Some Risk 4–7 At Risk below 4	Goal: 25–35 Established ≥ 25 Emerging 10–24 Deficit < 10	Move to PSF
	PSF		Goal: 18 correct phonemes Low Risk 18 Some Risk 7–17 At Risk < 7	Goal: 35 correct phonemes Established 35–45 Emerging 10–34 Deficit < 10
Letter Recognition	LNF	Goal: 8 correct letters Low Risk ≥ 8 Some Risk 2–7 At Risk < 2	Goal: 27 correct letters Low Risk ≥ 27 Some Risk 15–26 At Risk < 15	Goal: 40 correct letters Low Risk ≥ 40 Some Risk 29–39 At Risk < 29
Alphabetic Principle/ Phonics	NWF		Goal 13 correct letter sounds Low Risk ≥ 13 Some Risk 5–12 At Risk < 5	Goal 25 correct letter sounds Low Risk ≥ 25 Some Risk 15–24 At Risk < 15
Vocabulary	WUF	Low Risk > 20th percentile for your district or class At Risk ≤ 20th percentile for your district or class	Low Risk > 20th percentile for your district or class At Risk ≤ 20th percentile for your district or class	Low Risk > 20th percentile for your district or class At Risk ≤ 20th percentile for your district or class

Introduction

Aligning the DIBELS Screening Schedule with TREASURES
First Grade

TREASURES	DIBELS Measure	Unit 1/ Beginning	Unit 3/ Middle	Unit 5/ End
Letter Recognition	LNF	Goal: 37 correct letters Low Risk ≥ 37 Some Risk 25–36 At Risk < 25		
Phonemic Awareness	PSF	Goal: 35 correct Phonemes Established 35–45 Emerging 10–34 Deficit < 10	Goal: 35 correct phonemes Established 35–45 Emerging 10–34 Deficit < 10	Goal: 35 correct phonemes Established 35–45 Emerging 10–34 Deficit < 10
Alphabetic Principle/ Phonics	NWF	Goal: 24 correct sounds Low Risk ≥ 24 Some Risk 13–23 At Risk 13	Goal: 50 correct sounds and 15 words recoded Established ≥ 50 ≥ 15 words recoded Emerging 30–49 < 15 words recoded Deficit < 30 < 15 words recoded	Goal: 50 correct sounds and 15 words recoded Established ≥ 50 ≥ 15 words recoded Emerging 30–49 < 15 words recoded Deficit < 30 < 15 words recoded
Fluency	ORF		Goal: 20 correct words per minute Low Risk > 20 Some Risk 8–19 At Risk ≤ 7	Goal: 40 correct words per minute Low Risk > 40 Some Risk 20–39 At Risk < 19
Comprehension	RTF		Goal: 50% of ORF score Low Risk > 25% At Risk ≤ 25%	Goal: 50% of ORF score Low Risk > 25% At Risk ≤ 25%
Vocabulary	WUF	Low Risk > 20th percentile At Risk ≤ 20th percentile	Low Risk > 20th percentile At Risk ≤ 20th percentile	Low Risk > 20th percentile At Risk ≤ 20th percentile

Diagnostic Assessment

Aligning the DIBELS Screening Schedule with TREASURES
Second Grade

TREASURES	DIBELS Measure	Unit 1/ Beginning	Unit 3/ Middle	Unit 5/ End
Alphabetic Principle/ Phonics	NWF	Goal: 50 correct sounds and 15 words recoded Low Risk ≥ 50 ≥ 15 words recoded Some Risk 30–49 < 15 words recoded At Risk < 30 < 15 words recoded		
Fluency	ORF	Goal: 44 correct words per minute Low Risk > 44 Some Risk 26–43 At Risk ≤ 25	Goal: 68 correct words per minute Low Risk > 68 Some Risk 52–67 At Risk < 51	Goal: 90 correct words per minute Low Risk > 90 Some Risk 70–89 At Risk < 69
Comprehension	RTF	Goal: 50% of ORF score Low Risk > 25% of ORF Score At Risk ≤ 25% of ORF score	Goal: 50% of ORF score Low Risk > 25% of ORF Score At Risk ≤ 25% of ORF score	Goal: 50% of ORF score Low Risk > 25% of ORF Score At Risk ≤ 25% of ORF score
Vocabulary	WUF	Low Risk > 20th percentile for your district or class At Risk ≤ 20th percentile for your district or class	Low Risk > 20th percentile for your district or class At Risk ≤ 20th percentile for your district or class	Low Risk > 20th percentile for your district or class At Risk ≤ 20th percentile for your district or class

Introduction

Aligning the DIBELS Screening Schedule with TREASURES

Third Grade

TREASURES	DIBELS Measure	Unit 1/ Beginning	Unit 3/ Middle	Unit 5/ End
Fluency	ORF	Goal: 77 correct words per minute Low Risk ≥ 77 Some Risk 53–76 At Risk ≤ 52	Goal: 92 correct words per minute Low Risk ≥ 92 Some Risk 67–91 At Risk ≤ 66	Goal: 110 correct words per minute Low Risk ≥ 110 Some Risk 80–109 At Risk ≤ 79
Comprehension	RTF	Goal: 50% of ORF score Low Risk > 25% of ORF Score At Risk ≤ 25% of ORF score	Goal: 50% of ORF score Low Risk > 25% of ORF Score At Risk ≤ 25% of ORF score	Goal: 50% of ORF score Low Risk > 25% of ORF Score At Risk ≤ 25% of ORF score
Vocabulary	WUF	Low Risk > 20th percentile for your district or class At Risk ≤ 20th percentile for your district or class	Low Risk > 20th percentile for your district or class At Risk ≤ 20th percentile for your district or class	Low Risk > 20th percentile for your district or class At Risk ≤ 20th percentile for your district or class

Introduction

Using <u>TPRI</u> for Screening

What is the TPRI screening assessment?

- The Texas Primary Reading Inventory is a teacher-administered assessment that quickly identifies students who are NOT at risk of reading failure.

- It allows teachers to target their instruction and resources on those students who need further evaluation.

- It is a predictive assessment.

What does it do?

- The TPRI is designed to supplement and facilitate teacher judgment.

- It identifies students as developed or still developing literacy concepts.

How does it work?

- The screening test is a series of short (i.e. in three–five minutes), student-friendly tasks.

- The Kindergarten screening is administered in Mid-January and Mid-April.

- The Grade 1 screening is administered in Mid-September and Mid-April.

- The Grade 2 screening is administered in Mid-September.

- The Grade 3 screening is administered in Mid-September.

What do they measure?

- **Graphophonemic Knowledge:** the recognition of alphabet letters and the understanding of sound-symbol relationships.

- **Phonemic Awareness:** the ability to identify, think about, or manipulate the individual sounds in words.

- **Word Reading:** the correct identification of words. Students are identified as *Developed* or *Still Developing*.

Diagnostic Assessment

Introduction

How to Sequence the <u>TPRI</u> Kit

Step 1: Screening Section

- All students take the screening assessment.

- Allows you to identify students who are not likely to experience difficultly learning to read.

- Provides a way to focus additional resources on students who need more evaluation.

Step 2: Inventory Section

- Students who are *Still Developing* move on to the Inventory Section.

- Optional: Administer to all students for additional diagnostic information.

Step 3: Reading Accuracy, Fluency, and Comprehension (Listening Comprehension in Grade K)

- Administer to all students.

Aligning the <u>TPRI</u> Screening Schedule with <u>TREASURES</u>

Kindergarten

    Unit 4/Mid-Year: Phonemic Awareness, Graphophonemic Knowledge

    Unit 9/End of Year: Phonemic Awareness, Graphophonemic Knowledge

First Grade

    Unit 1/Beginning of Year: Phonemic Awareness, Graphophonemic Knowledge, and Word Reading

    Unit 5/End of Year: Phonemic Awareness and Word Reading

Second Grade

    Unit 1/Beginning of Year: Word Reading

Third Grade

    Unit 1/Beginning of Year: Word Reading

Introduction

Administering the <u>TPRI</u> Screening Assessment

1. Read the directions before beginning.

2. Begin with the practice items.

3. Administer the task to the student.

4. Be sure to pronounce the phonemes correctly.

5. Follow the Branching Rules.

6. Scoring criteria:
   Developed or *Still Developing*

7. Grade 2: Students who are identified as still developing on the TPRI screening at the beginning of grade 2 may be in need of intensive reading intervention.

8. Grade 3: The screening tasks should be simplified into one task. Administer all twenty items at one time. This makes it easier to administer and evaluate.

9. Third-grade students who do not read at least nineteen out of twenty words correctly on the combined tasks are at risk of falling below the 20th percentile on a standardized, end-of-the-year, reading test.

Diagnostic Assessment

Introduction

Diagnostic Options

Diagnostic Assessments

There are several diagnostic assessments you can use for identifying the strengths and weaknesses of your students. These can be used according to a schedule or at any time during the year when in-depth information about a student is needed.

TPRI (Texas Primary Reading Inventory), K-3

For developing students, the Inventory portion of the **TPRI** allows teachers to gather specific diagnostic information. The Inventory section measures:

- Book and Print Awareness (K)
- Phonemic Awareness (K–1)
- Listening Comprehension (K–1)
- Graphophonemic Knowledge (K–3)
- Reading Accuracy (1–3)
- Reading Fluency (1–3)
- Reading Comprehension (1–3)

Informal Reading Inventory, 1-6

IRIs are silent and oral reading passages that are used to determine students' Independent, Instructional, and Frustrational reading levels. Students read successively more difficult, grade-level text, and answer vocabulary and comprehension questions.

Placement, K-6

Use a combination of the skill-specific tests included in this book to help make decisions about placing students in the *Treasures* program. The Placement Decision Charts on pages 6–11 provide cut scores and guidelines for decision making.

Introduction

Using <u>TPRI</u> as a Diagnostic

What is the TPRI Inventory assessment?

- The Inventory is a diagnostic tool intended to guide instruction.
- The Inventory reveals students' strengths and weaknesses to help teachers plan differentiated classroom instruction.

What does it do?

- It gives teachers an opportunity to acquire more data to help match reading instruction with specific student needs.

How does it work?

- The Inventory is administered to all students who fail the screening section.
- It takes about twenty minutes to administer and materials are color coded.
- Concepts are considered *Developed* when students provide correct responses to the indicated number of items within a task. Teachers then proceed to the next task.
- If a student does not respond to the indicated number of items, the concept is considered *Still Developing.*
- At the beginning of the year, students are expected to score *Still Developing* on many of the Inventory tasks; they are expected to learn and develop the skills measured on the Inventory throughout the school year.

What does it measure?

- **Book and Print Awareness/Concepts of Print:** The ability to concentrate on the conventions and formats of print.
- **Phonemic Awareness:** The ability to attend to the sound structure of spoken language.
- **Graphophonemic Knowledge:** The ability to recognize letters and understand sound-spelling relationships.
- **Listening and Reading Comprehension:** Word lists help place students into the appropriate instructional reading level.
- **Reading Accuracy and Reading Fluency**

Diagnostic Assessment

Introduction

Inventory Branching Rules

- All tasks are arranged from easiest to most difficult.

- A basic task is the first or easiest one, and an advanced task is the last or hardest one.

- Begin with the easiest task and stay within the same portion of the Inventory as long as the student continues to score as *Developed*.

- If a student scores *Still Developing* on a task, stop and move the student to the next portion of the Inventory.

How to Prevent Student Frustration

- If the student is reading the entire passage at a Frustrational Level, stop and ask the student to read the previous passage instead.

- At Grades 1 and 2, the Frustrational Level is defined as the point when the student cannot read three or more words in the *first* sentence.

- In Grade 1, the teacher can read the story aloud and treat this as Listening Comprehension.

- In Grade 2, the teacher should administer the First Grade Word List before going back to a first-grade story.

Aligning the <u>TPRI</u> Inventory Schedule with <u>TREASURES</u>

Kindergarten

Unit 4/Middle of the Year and **Unit 9**/End of the Year:
Book and Print Awareness, Phonemic Awareness, Graphophonemic Knowledge, Reading/Listening Comprehension

First Grade

Unit 1/Beginning of Year, **Unit 3**/Middle of Year, and **Unit 5**/End of Year:
Phonemic Awareness, Graphophonemic Knowledge, Reading Accuracy, Fluency, and Reading/Listening Comprehension

Second and Third Grades

Unit 1/Beginning of Year, **Unit 3**/Middle of Year, and **Unit 5**/End of Year:
Graphophonemic Knowledge, Reading Accuracy, Fluency, and Reading/Listening Comprehension

Introduction

Other Assessment Opportunities

Assessment is an ongoing and continuous process. It does not end after you administer diagnostic and screening tests and assessments for placement. In fact, good teaching requires that you teach and assess simultaneously, thereby providing immediate corrective feedback and lesson modifications. The following pages detail how informal assessments can be used to confirm (or not) diagnostic assessment results and can lead you to administer additional diagnostic assessments based on observed student needs.

Informal Assessments

The reading classroom is full of assessment opportunities. Chances are you use some of them without realizing you are doing "assessment." Remember the definition of assessment is systematically gathering information about what students know and can do. In reading, you can do this in an informal way throughout instruction.

- **Teach students to monitor their own comprehension.** Monitoring comprehension is an important comprehension strategy explicitly taught in **TREASURES** from Grades one through six. Students can ask themselves questions about what they have just read. Good readers learn to use these metacognitive skills unconsciously. Have you ever said to yourself, "I am not sure what I just read"? Your automatic monitoring system helps you improve your comprehension of the text.

- **Ask students to retell** or explain in their own words what they have just read. A good explanation shows you what a student understands, and a poor explanation makes the student's misconceptions and misunderstandings apparent so you can address them.

- **Teach students how to monitor their own progress.** If children realize they do not understand something they have read, they can try various reading strategies and/or ask for help from peers or from their teacher. Listen for the substance of the answer, and not merely if it is "correct" or not. Learn from the student's answer what he or she is thinking.

Diagnostic Assessment

Introduction

Types of Informal Assessments

Quick Checks: TREASURES provides many opportunities for you to observe students independently practice a strategy or skill taught in whole group instruction.

- The Quick Check reminds you to observe your students and see if any of them are having difficulty with a skill they have just learned.

- You can use this information to decide if this is a skill you need to address in small group instruction.

Assignments: Every assignment or activity allows you to assess reading behaviors. Assignments do not need to be formally graded, but they should be treated as a potential source of information about what students know, what they still need to learn, and what their misconceptions or difficulties are.

- Review assignments, noting both strengths and weaknesses, and present the student with oral or written feedback.

- Ask students to go over their own assignments in groups, where peers can point out their strengths and weaknesses to each other. Note that this is an opportunity to show students that looking at what is right and wrong is important.

- Ask students to go over their own work and reflect upon it. This, too, is a skill that needs to be modeled and taught.

Classroom Observations: You have opportunities to observe your students at work and at play, working alone, and interacting with other students. Be systematic with the way you do and record the observations.

- Does this student like to read or look at books? What topics is he or she interested in?

- How does this student work with others?

- You can ask students what kinds of stories or books they like. You should strive to create a print-rich environment, with materials at a wide range of reading levels on as many topics as possible. Expand on students' interests and introduce new ones.

Introduction

QUICK CHECKS OBSERVATIONS FORM (PRIMARY)					
Student's Name	Phonemic Awareness	Phonics	Fluency	Comprehension	Vocabulary

Diagnostic Assessment

Introduction

QUICK CHECKS OBSERVATIONS FORM (INTERMEDIATE)				
Student's Name	Phonics/Word Study	Fluency	Comprehension	Vocabulary

Diagnostic Assessment

Phonemic Awareness

- ## Phonological Awareness Screening Test
    1. Detecting Rhymes
    2. Counting Syllables
    3. Matching Initial Sounds
    4. Counting Phonemes
    5. Comparing Word Lengths
    6. Representing Phonemes with Letters

- ## Distinguishing Initial, Final, Medial Sounds
- ## Phoneme Segmentation Fluency
- ## Phoneme Deletion Test
- ## Sound Substitution

Phonological Awareness Screening Test

▶ **WHAT** The *Phonological Awareness Screening Test* contains six subtests:

1. Detecting Rhymes

2. Counting Syllables

3. Matching Initial Sounds

4. Counting Phonemes

5. Comparing Word Lengths

6. Representing Phonemes with Letters

The test can be administered to groups of students or on an individual basis. Students are led through a series of tasks by the teacher in which they indicate their answers by connecting pictures with lines, circling pictures, writing tally marks, or writing letters. Students unfamiliar with these types of tasks should receive practice in completing such tasks prior to administration of this assessment.

This test is best used in conjunction with ongoing training in phonemic awareness.

▶ **WHY** Since phonemic awareness has been identified as a crucial pre-skill for learning to read, early assessment is important. Use this assessment for screening phonological awareness skills in groups of students. By administering the test to everyone in your class, you can objectively estimate your students' level of phonological awareness. The assessment can also help to identify students whose lack of phonological awareness may be causing difficulty in their acquisition of reading and spelling skills. This test should be administered as a screening tool to all kindergarten students mid-year and to all first-graders in the fall and only to second-graders who are not yet reading.

Phonemic Awareness Grades K–3

▶ **HOW** When testing kindergartners, group size should be kept to a maximum of six students; groups of two or three are preferable. Group size should not exceed 15 for first-graders. Also, it is helpful to have a second adult involved to ensure that students are on task.

Each student should have a pencil and a test booklet made by compiling the student testing forms that appear on the following pages. You should have ready access to the demonstration pages, a copy of the student booklet, and a pencil or marker to use for demonstration.

The pages that follow provide a description of each subtest along with subtest administration and scoring directions. The directions are followed by the demonstration page and the student test form for that subtest.

▶ **WHAT IT MEANS** As a rule of thumb, a high score indicates that a student is progressing well on the capabilities tested. A student may obtain a low score, however, on any or all subtests for reasons wholly unrelated to their content or purpose. Students who perform poorly on any subtest should be further assessed on a one-to-one basis.

Each subtest has a maximum possible score of 5. It is helpful to average the scores for the entire class. An average score of 4.0 indicates that the corresponding section of the curriculum should be revisited. If the average score is less than 3.0, the corresponding section of the curriculum warrants more serious attention. Also, find time to sit down with any students whose score falls 2 or more points beneath the class average on any given subtest so that you can discover whether they are indeed in need of extra help and practice.

Since each subtest measures a key phonological awareness task, information obtained can help determine instructional focus. Normally progressing kindergarten students should be able to detect rhymes, count syllables, and match initial sounds by the middle of kindergarten. By the end of kindergarten or early first grade, students will be able to count phonemes and compare word lengths. By the middle to end of first grade, most students should be able to represent phonemes with letters.

▶ **WHAT'S NEXT?** Students who are able to match initial sounds will profit from phonics instruction. Students who do not meet any of the expected benchmarks noted above in "What It Means" will benefit from more intensive phonemic awareness training and more language work in general. An intervention of about 14 hours of phonemic awareness instruction (3–4 days a week for 15–20 minutes for about ten weeks) is all that is needed by many students in Grades K–2. ***Reading Triumphs*** is a highly effective intervention program. You can also use the lessons provided in the ***Treasures*** **Phonemic Awareness Teacher's Edition**.

For most students, the ability to detect and produce rhymes seems to develop without formal instruction. Nevertheless, research shows sensitivity to rhyme to be a useful indicator of a basic entry level of phonological awareness (Lundberg, Olofsson, & Wall, 1980; Muter, 1994). That is, to appreciate the similarity between the words *hat* and *cat*, the student must shift attention from the meanings of words to the sounds of words. Although solid sensitivity to rhyme does not lead automatically or directly to phonemic awareness, its absence suggests trouble and warrants instructional response.

DESCRIPTION

On the test form, there are ten pictures. For each picture in the left column, there is another picture on the page with a rhyming name. The student's task is to connect the rhyming pictures by drawing lines between them.

ADMINISTRATION

Begin by explaining that two words rhyme when they sound similar at the end and give the students several examples of rhyming words:

cheek - peek
chair - hair
most - toast

Prompt the students to think of a few more rhymes:

Can anyone think of a word that rhymes with bed? . . . *with* lace? *(e.g., face, race) . . . with* toy? *(e.g., boy, joy) . . . with* king? *(e.g., sing, ring)*

Then hold up your demonstration page, which shows two columns of two pictures each, and point to the first picture on the left:

Can you name this picture?

Yes, it is a clock. *Now look at the pictures on this side of the page. Can you find one that rhymes with* clock? *Raise your hands if you know.*

Phonemic Awareness Grades K–3

Very good, clock and sock rhyme. Listen: clock . . . sock.

To show that these two pictures rhyme, I will draw a line between them.

Demonstrate again, making sure all attend.

Turn to the first page of your booklet. Here you have ten pictures. Every picture in the left row rhymes with another picture somewhere on the page.

Find the rhyming words and connect them by drawing a line from one to the other.

Before you begin, I will tell you the names of the pictures.

Pointing to one picture at a time from top to bottom and left to right, name each clearly, making sure that all students attend and understand:

Tree, moon, house, cat, car, mouse, hat, spoon, star, bee.

Okay. Now you start looking for the rhymes. Don't forget to draw a line between pictures that rhyme.

When you have finished, put down your pencil and look at me.

SCORING

Give each student 1 point for each correctly matched pair so that the maximum possible score is 5.

Answers: tree-bee; moon-spoon; house-mouse; cat-hat; car-star

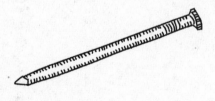

Phonemic Awareness Grades K–3

Research shows that the ability to attend to syllables is easier than the ability to attend to phonemes and, furthermore, that syllabic awareness generally emerges earlier than phonemic awareness in the student's development (Lundberg, Frost, & Petersen, 1988). This subtest assesses students' phonemic awareness by asking them to count the number of syllables in different words.

DESCRIPTION

The test form shows five pictures, each followed by a blank response line. The students must indicate the number of syllables in each of the pictured words by writing as many tallies on the response line.

ADMINISTRATION

Begin by showing the students how to count the number of syllables in words. By clapping as you enunciate each syllable, demonstrate words (*e.g., far-mer, nap-kin, sand-wich*) that consist of two syllables. Mark the syllables by clapping hands. Similarly, a few three-syllable words (e.g., *am-bu-lance, bi-cy-cle, ham-bur-ger*) should be clapped and counted. A few monosyllabic words should also be demonstrated (e.g., *book, car, soup*). Then hold up your demonstration page and point to the first picture:

Look at this picture. What is it?

Yes, it is a window. *Now we say the word slowly and in syllables:* win-dow.

Let's say this word together slowly, so we can hear the syllables: al-li-ga-tor. *How many syllables?*

Yes, four. So what should I do?

Yes, I should make four marks in the space next to the alligator.

Phonemic Awareness Grades K-3

Demonstrate and display your four tally marks. Again, pronounce the word *alligator*, syllable by syllable, pointing to the four marks in turn as you do so. Now ask the students to look at their test page.

What do you think you have to do on this page?

Yes. For each picture, you must see if you can figure out how many syllables are in the name of each picture you see.

Before you begin, I will name each picture here.

Listen carefully: pencil, elephant, motorcycle, bow, helicopter.

See if you can count the syllables for each picture. Be sure to mark the number of syllables next to each picture.

When you have finished, put down your pencil and look at me.

SCORING

Give each student 1 point for each correctly identified number of syllables so that the maximum possible score is 5.

Answers: pencil (2); elephant (3); motorcycle (4); bow (1); helicopter (4)

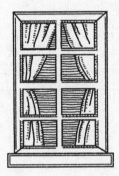

_____

_____

Phonemic Awareness Grades K–3

Research shows that the ability to judge whether words have the same first sounds is a critical first step in the development of phonemic awareness. This subtest assesses this ability by asking the students to match items that begin with the same phoneme.

DESCRIPTION

The test form shows ten pictures. For every picture in the left column, there is one somewhere else on the page that begins with exactly the same phoneme. The students are to connect items that begin with the same sound by drawing a line between them.

ADMINISTRATION

Hold up your demonstration page and point to the top left picture so that all can see.

Look at this picture. This is a picture of a seal.

What is the first sound of the word seal? *Raise your hand if you know.*

Yes, the first sound of seal *is* /s-s-s-s-s/: s-s-s-seal.

Now direct the students' attention to the column of pictures on the right side of the page.

Now look at the pictures on this side of the page. Can you find one that begins with the same first sound as seal? *If you can, raise your hand.*

Good. Sun *starts with the same sound as* seal. *Listen carefully:* s-s-s-sun . . . s-s-s-seal.

Now we draw a line between seal *and* sun *to show that they begin with the same sound.*

Draw a line between the two pictures to demonstrate, holding up the page to make sure that all see and understand. Then direct the students' attention to the bottom left picture.

Here is a picture of a kite. *What is the first sound of the word* kite? *Raise your hand if you know.*

Yes, the first sound of kite *is* /k/: k-k-kite.

Phonemic Awareness Grades K–3

Redirect the students' attention to the column of pictures on the right side of the page.

Do you see a picture over here that begins with the same sound as kite?

Yes, king *begins with /k/. Listen:* k-k-kite, k-k-king.

Draw a line between the two pictures so that all the students can see what you have done. Now ask the students to turn to the test page. Pointing to each column in turn, explain the following:

For every picture on this side, see if you can find another over here that begins with the same sound.

When you find two pictures that begin with the same sound, draw a line between them.

Before you begin, I will tell you the name of each picture.

Point to each picture, top to bottom and left to right, as you name it.

Listen carefully: lamp, pig, fork, balloon, heart, bird, feather, hand, leaf, pencil.

Find the pictures that start with the same sound and draw a line between them.

When you have finished, you can put down your pencil and look at me. Okay, go ahead!

SCORING

Give each student 1 point for each correctly matched pair so that the maximum possible score is 5.

Answers: lamp-leaf; pig-pencil; fork-feather; balloon-bird; heart-hand

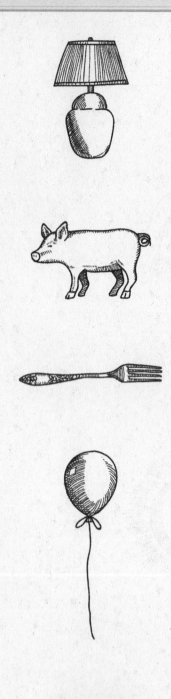

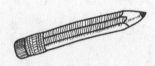

Phonemic Awareness Grades K–3

This subtest requires the students to count the number of sounds or phonemes in different words. Research has demonstrated that this task is highly correlated to other tasks on phonemic awareness. It is also a good predictor of reading achievement (Hoien, Lundberg, Stanovich, & Bjaalid, 1995).

DESCRIPTION

The test page presents five pictures, each followed by a blank response space. The students are to count the number of phonemes in the words depicted by each picture and to indicate their answers, with tally marks, in the accompanying response space.

ADMINISTRATION

Hold up your demonstration page and point to the first picture.

Here is a picture of a knee. *Say the word* knee *very slowly to yourselves. How many sounds do you hear?* (It is the number of phonemes, not the number of letters that is of interest here.)

Let's try it together. /n/ . . . /ē/. *How many sounds?*

Yes, two: /n/ . . . /ē/.

To show that knee *has two sounds, I have to put two marks here on the line next to its picture.*

Making sure that all of the students can see and are paying attention, put two tally marks (II) next to the picture of a knee on the demonstration page. Then review your solution, pointing to each mark in turn as you voice the phoneme it represents: /n/ . . . /ē/.

What does the next picture show?

Yes, the sun. *How many sounds in the word* sun?

Let's try it together: /s/ . . . /u/ . . . /n/. *How many? Good, three. So what should I do next?*

Good, I have to write three marks in the space next to the sun.

Again making sure that all of the students can see and are paying attention, put three tally marks (III) next to the picture of the sun on the demonstration page. Then review, pointing to each mark in turn as you voice the phoneme it represents: /s/ . . . /u/ . . . /n/. Now ask the students to turn to their test page, and continue:

There are pictures of five things here. You must try to mark how many sounds are in the name of each picture.

Before you begin, let me name the pictures for you.

Point to each picture in turn while carefully enunciating its name:

Toe, ant, broom, soap, paste.

When you figure out the number of sounds in each word, make the same number of marks beside it.

When you are finished, put down your pencil and look at me.

SCORING

Give each student 1 point for each correctly identified number of sounds so that the maximum possible score is 5.

Answers:

toe (2): /t/ . . . /ō/

ant (3): /a/ . . . /n/ . . . /t/

broom (4): /b/ . . . /r/ . . . /o͞o/ . . . /m/

soap (3): /s/ . . . /ō/ . . . /p/

paste (4): /p/ . . . /ā/ . . . /s/ . . . /t/

Diagnostic Assessment

_____

_____

_____

_____

_____

_____

_____

Diagnostic Assessment

Phonemic Awareness Grades K–3

In this task, the students have to compare two words and decide which of them is made up of the greatest number of phonemes. Successful performance requires that the students ignore the meanings of the words, attending only to their phonemic structure.

DESCRIPTION

The test page presents five pairs of pictures. For each set, the students are to circle the picture that represents the word with the greatest number of phonemes.

ADMINISTRATION

Hold up your demonstration page and point to the first pair of pictures:

Look at the first pair of pictures. One shows a bow *and the other shows a* boat. *I need to circle the picture that has more sounds. Which of these two pictures should I circle? Raise your hand if you know.*

Let's say both words slowly and compare them: bow . . . /b/ . . . /ō/. *How many sounds does* bow *have? Yes, two.*

Now let's try boat: /b/. . . /ō/. . . /t/. *How many sounds does* boat *have? Yes, three.*

So which picture should I circle? Which one has more sounds?

Yes, boat *has more sounds than* bow. *Listen carefully:* boat . . . bow.

Making sure that all are paying attention, circle the picture of the boat. Then repeat the demonstration with the second pair of pictures, *nail* and *snail*:

Look at the second pair of pictures. One shows a snail *and the other shows a* nail. *I need to circle the picture that has more sounds. Which of these two pictures should I circle? Raise your hand if you know.*

Let's say both words slowly and compare them: snail . . . /s/ . . . /n/ . . . /ā/ . . . /l/. *How many sounds does* snail *have? Yes, four.*

Phonemic Awareness Grades K–3

Now let's try nail: /n/ . . . /ā/ . . . /l/. *How many sounds does* nail *have? Yes, three.*

So which picture should I circle? Which one has more sounds?

Then ask the children to turn to the test page.

Here are five pairs of pictures. For each pair, you must circle the one that has the most sounds.

Let me first name them all for you: card, car; bed, bread; bus, brush; crown, cow; eye, fly.

Remember: for each pair, circle the picture whose name has the most sounds.

SCORING

Give each student 1 point for each correctly identified word so that the maximum possible score is 5.

Answers:

card (3): /k/ . . . /ar/ . . . /d/
bread (4): /b/ . . . /r/ . . . /e/ . . . /d/
brush (4): /b/ . . . /r/ . . . /u/ . . . /sh/
crown (4): /k/ . . . /r/ . . . /ou/ . . . /n/
fly (3): /f/ . . . /l/ . . . /ī/

Diagnostic Assessment

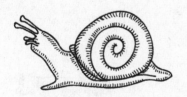

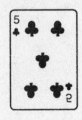

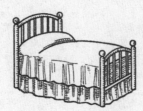

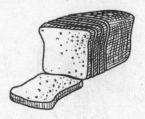

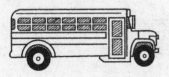

Phonemic Awareness Grades K–3

This final task challenges students to combine their phonemic awareness and letter knowledge to spell words independently. Because it is students' understanding of the alphabetic principle that is of interest, all of the words involve simple, direct sound-to-letter mappings. Such alphabetic understanding is strongly related to learning to read (Hatcher, Hulme, & Ellis, 1994).

DESCRIPTION

The test form presents five pictures, and the students are asked to spell the name of each.

ADMINISTRATION

Hold up your demonstration page and point to the first picture.

Here is a picture of a bat. *Do you think you can spell* bat? *Let's try together.*

Let's start by saying the word bat *very slowly, sound by sound:* /b/-/a/-/t/. *What is the first sound? So what letter do we write first?*

Making sure all of the students are paying attention, write the letter *b* in the space next to the picture of the bat.

Okay. What is the second sound of the word bat? *Listen carefully:* /b/-/a/-/t/.

Which letter do we write for /a/? *Good, it's the letter* a.

Add the letter *a*. Then, to show that the word is still incomplete, sound what you have spelled thus far as you point to the letters:

/b/-/a/ . . . That's not enough. What else do we need?

Let's listen again: /b/-/a/-/t/. *Which letter do we write for* /t/? *Yes,* t.

Add the letter *t* and then, left to right as you point to the letters, sound your spelling to show that it is complete and correct. Then ask the students to turn to their test pages. Before asking them to begin, name each of the pictured words for them: *sun, mop, pot, frog, nest.*

SCORING

Each word should be scored as either correct or incorrect, yielding a maximum possible score of 5 points. Independently of the larger test, the results from this subtest may be rescored for analysis of the students' spelling growth per se. For this purpose, a student should be given 1 point for each sound that is correctly represented, provided that left-to-right order is not violated. As an example, using the word *nest*:

4 points	nest
3 points	nst, net, nes, nist, nust, nustu
2 points	nset, ns, nt, nat
1 point	n

When scored in this way, the maximum number of points on this subtest is 17. The students' scores should be reviewed to identify any who are significantly behind their classmates so that they can be given extra help.

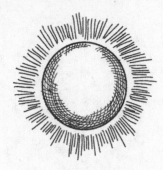

_____

_____

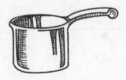

_____

_____

_____

Diagnostic Assessment

Distinguishing Initial, Medial, and Final Sounds

This phonemic awareness test assesses a child's ability to perceive and distinguish sounds in words. Read each word aloud. Ask the child to name the target sound (initial, medial, or final). Record the child's response on the blank. Circle each correct response. Then tally the total number correct. A score of 4 or higher on each subtest indicates proficiency with the skill. A score below 4 indicates that the child may need additional instruction and practice.

Initial Sounds

"Say the first, or beginning, sound in each word."

1. sad ____
2. fish ____
3. top ____
4. ball ____
5. yes ____

Score ____/5

Final Sounds

"Say the last, or final, sound in each word."

1. rat ____
2. bed ____
3. fell ____
4. crib ____
5. pig ____

Score ____/5

Medial Sounds

"Say the middle, or medial, sound in each word."

1. rain ____
2. boat ____
3. cat ____
4. him ____
5. red ____

Score ____/5

Distinguishing Sounds
Initial Sounds

"Listen to the three words. Which word begins with a different sound?"

1. map, man, ham ____
2. leaf, fell, lips ____
3. pen, nest, note ____
4. dog, big, door ____
5. vine, van, fish ____

Score ____/5

Final Sounds

"Listen to the three words. Which word ends with a different sound?"

1. pan, pet, run ____
2. fed, let, hot ____
3. bell, hill, win ____
4. leaf, like, roof ____
5. rob, tip, rope ____

Score ____/5

Medial Sounds

"Listen to the three words. Which word has a different sound in the middle?"

1. feet, need, fight ____
2. coat, hot, road ____
3. sun, nest, rug ____
4. him, his, set ____
5. leg, bag, fed ____

Score ____/5

Phoneme Segmentation Fluency Assessment

Instructions for Administering Phoneme Segmentation

1. Make a copy of the Phoneme Segmentation Fluency record sheet. Use this sheet to record student's oral responses.

2. Say these directions to the student:

   I am going to say a word. Then, you tell me all the sounds you hear in the word. So if I say, "cat" you will say /k/ /a/ /t/. Let's try one. Tell me all the sounds in "hop."

3. If the student gives the correct response, /h/ /o/ /p/, then commend the student.

4. If the student gives an incorrect response, say: *The sounds in "hop" are* /h/ /o/ /p/. Ask the student to repeat the sounds: *Tell me all the sounds in "hop."*

5. Give the student the first word and start your stopwatch. Place a check above each correct sound segment produced. Put a slash (/) through incorrect sounds.

6. The maximum time for each sound segment is 3 seconds. If the student does not provide the next sound segment within 3 seconds, give the student the next word.

7. At the end of 1 minute, stop presenting words and scoring further responses. Add the number of sound segments produced correctly. Record the total number of sound segments produced correctly on the bottom of the scoring sheet.

Directions for Scoring

1. If the student has not given any sound segments correctly in the first 5 words, discontinue the task and put a score of zero. (0)

2. Place a check above the sound segments in the word that are correctly pronounced by the student. The student receives 1 point for each correct part of the word.

   Both of the following examples are correct segmentations of words:

Word	Student Response	Scoring Procedure	Correct Segments
like	"l…i…k"	/l/ /ī/ /k/	3/3
crack	"k..r..a..k"	/k/ /r/ /a/ /k/	4/4

3. Put a slash through segments pronounced incorrectly.

4. See the **Phoneme Segmentation Fluency Growth Table** on page 6 of the Letter Naming and Sight Words section to obtain a phoneme segmentation fluency score.

Phonemic Awareness Grades K–3

Name _____ Date _____

Record Sheet

Phoneme Segmentation Fluency		# correct
man /m/ /a/ /n/	thing /th/ /i/ /ng/	___ /6
his /h/ /i/ /z/	kiss /k/ /i/ /s/	___ /6
brand /b/ /r/ /a/ /n/ /d/	match /m/ /a/ /ch/	___ /8
smile /s/ /m/ /ī/ /l/	froze /f/ /r/ /ō/ /z/	___ /8
press /p/ /r/ /e/ /s/	cheat /ch/ /ē/ /t/	___ /7
slope /s/ /l/ /ō/ /p/	tide /t/ /ī/ /d/	___ /7
blend /b/ /l/ /e/ /n/ /d/	gate /g/ /ā/ /t/	___ /8
lost /l/ /o/ /s/ /t/	shop /sh/ /o/ /p/	___ /7
jump /j/ /u/ /m/ /p/	drill /d/ /r/ /i/ /l/	___ /8
those /th/ /ō/ /s/	west /w/ /e/ /s/ /t/	___ /7
plug /p/ /l/ /u/ /g/	rush /r/ /u/ /sh/	___ /7
tape /t/ /ā/ /p/	inch /i/ /n/ /ch/	___ /6

Phoneme Deletion Test

▶ **WHAT** This assessment includes four phoneme deletion tasks arranged in order of difficulty. The first task assesses the student's ability to delete initial phonemes. For example, the examiner may say the word *cat* and ask the student to say *cat* without the initial /k/ sound. The remaining tasks assess the student's ability to delete final phonemes, such as /t/ in the word *seat*; initial phonemes in blends, such as /s/ in the word *slip*; and phonemes embedded in blends, such as /l/ in the word *play*. The assessment contains minimal grade-level expectations for Grades 1 to 3, but can also be used with older students.

▶ **WHY** These tasks may help to determine whether deficits in phonemic, or sound, awareness account for the student's reading or spelling delays. According to research, the lack of phonemic awareness is the most powerful determinant of the likelihood of a student's failure to learn to read.

▶ **HOW** Before administering each task, administer the Practice Items. For all students, begin with the tasks in Part A of the test. Assess as far as the student can go, regardless of his or her grade placement. Do not correct errors; instead encourage students by praising their willingness to participate. Remember that this is an auditory assessment—students do not see the items on the test. The Correct Response column tells how the student's answer should sound, not how it should be spelled.

Diagnostic Assessment

Phonemic Awareness Grades K–3

PART A

Initial Sound
(Late K and Grade 1)

Begin by saying to the student, "We are going to play a word game. This game will give me information to help teach you better." Then administer the following two Practice Items.

Practice Item 1

TEACHER: Say *cat*.

STUDENT: *cat*

TEACHER: Now say it without the /k/.

STUDENT: *at*

If the student responds incorrectly say, "Let's try that again." For example, if the student says *kit*, model the correct response by emphasizing the /k/ and artificially separating it from the *at*. Help the student to give the correct response by saying each sound slowly. Repeat the Practice Item until the student gives the correct response—even if the student does not seem to understand the task. After the student repeats the correct response, proceed to Practice Item 2.

Practice Item 2

TEACHER: Say *table*.

STUDENT: *table*

TEACHER: Now say it without the /t/.

STUDENT: *able*

If the student responds incorrectly say, "Let's try that again." For example, if the student says *bull*, model the correct response by emphasizing the /t/ and artificially separating it from *able*. Encourage the student to repeat the correct response.

If the student can correctly respond to these two Practice Items, proceed to the Test Items. If the student cannot correctly respond to these Practice Items, skip Part A and proceed to the Practice Items for Part B. Some students may be able to delete a final sound, but not an initial sound.

Phonemic Awareness Grades K–3

PART B

Final Sound (Grade 1)

Say to the student, "We are going to play another word game. The rules of this game are a little different. Pay close attention." Then administer the following Practice Item.

Practice Item

TEACHER: Say *seat.*

STUDENT: *seat*

TEACHER: Now say it without the /t/.

STUDENT: *sea*

If the student responds incorrectly say, "Let's try that again." For example, if the student says *keat*, model the correct response by elongating *sea* and artificially separating it from the /t/. Then say, "*Seat* without the /t/ is *sea.*" Encourage the student to repeat the correct response.

If the student can correctly respond to the Practice Item, proceed to the Test Items. If the student cannot correctly respond to any of the Part A or B Practice Items, discontinue the assessment.

PART C

First Sound of a Consonant Blend (Grade 2)

Say to the student, "We are going to do something different now. Pay close attention." Then administer the following Practice Item.

Practice Item

TEACHER: Say *slip.*

STUDENT: *slip*

TEACHER: Now say it without the /s/.

STUDENT: *lip*

If the student responds incorrectly say, "Let's try that again." For example, if the student deletes the entire /sl/ blend and says *ip*, model a correct response by emphasizing the /s/ and separating it from *lip.* Say, "Be careful, you're taking off too much. Try to say it without the /s/." If necessary, help the student to repeat the correct response.

If the student can correctly respond to, or repeat, the Practice Item, proceed to the Test Items. If the student can respond correctly to at least two of the Test Items, proceed to Part D; otherwise, discontinue the assessment.

Diagnostic Assessment

PART D

Embedded Sound of a Consonant Blend (Grade 3)

Say to the student, "We are going to play another word game. The rules of this game are a little different." Then administer the following Practice Item.

Practice Item

TEACHER: Say *play*.

STUDENT: *play*

TEACHER: Now say it without the /l/.

STUDENT: *pay*

If the student responds incorrectly say, "Let's try that again." For example, if the student deletes the entire blend and says *ay*, say: "You are taking off too much. I just wanted you to say it without /l/." Model a correct response by separating all three sounds of the word: /p/ /l/ /ay/, and say: "Without the /l/ it is just /p/ /ay/—*pay*. So, what is *play* without the /l/? Yes, it is *pay*." If necessary, help the student to repeat the correct response.

If the student can correctly respond to, or repeat, the Practice Item, proceed to the Test Items.

▶ **WHAT IT MEANS** Use the guidelines below to determine the student's performance level.

Minimal Grade-Level Expectations

1–6 correct	late K / early Grade 1
7–10 correct	end of Grade 1
11–13 correct	early Grade 2
14–15 correct	end of Grade 2
16–18 correct	early Grade 3
19–20 correct	end of Grade 3

▶ **WHAT'S NEXT** Students who are able to do Part A: Initial Sound are especially ready for formal reading instruction. Students who do not meet grade expectations will benefit from more intense phonemic awareness instruction.

Phoneme Deletion Test

Name _____ Grade _____ Date _____

Directions: Follow the format used in the Practice Items to administer the items for each level. Mark "+" to indicate a correct response or "–" to indicate an incorrect response. Write down incorrect responses, but do not correct the student. If the student cannot complete any of the items in Parts A or B, discontinue testing. If the student cannot do at least two items in Part C, discontinue testing. Remember that this is an auditory assessment. Students do not see the items.

Part A: Initial Sound

Practice Items

Say *cat* ... now say it without the /k/ ___(at)

Say *table* ... now say it without the /t/ ___(able)

TEST ITEM		CORRECT RESPONSE	
1. (t)ower	our	(+) (-)	_____
2. (c)old	old	(+) (-)	_____
3. (b)ake	ache	(+) (-)	_____
4. (s)ize	eyes	(+) (-)	_____
5. (l)ow	owe	(+) (-)	_____

Part B: Final Sound

Practice Items

Say *seat* ... now say it without the /t/ ___(sea)

Say *rake* ... now say it without the /k/ ___(ray)

TEST ITEM		CORRECT RESPONSE	
6. to(n)e	toe	(+)(-)	_____
7. droo(p)	drew	(+)(-)	_____
8. ti(m)e	tie	(+)(-)	_____
9. ro(d)e	row	(+)(-)	_____
10. pla(c)e	play	(+)(-)	_____

Items Correct _____ **Grade Level** _____

Part C: First Sound of a Consonant Blend

Practice Items

Say *slip* ... now say it without the /s/ ___(lip)

Say *cloud* ... now say it without the /k/ ___(loud)

TEST ITEM		CORRECT RESPONSE	
11. (f)reight	rate	(+) (-)	_____
12. (p)layed	laid	(+) (-)	_____
13. (s)weet	wheat	(+) (-)	_____
14. (b)reak	rake	(+) (-)	_____
15. (s)pill	pill	(+) (-)	_____

Part D: Embedded Sound of a Consonant Blend

Practice Items

Say *slip* ... now say it without the /l/ ___(sip)

Say *play* ... now say it without the /l/ ___(pay)

TEST ITEM		CORRECT RESPONSE	
16. b(l)end	bend	(+)(-)	_____
17. t(w)in	tin	(+)(-)	_____
18. g(r)ow	go	(+)(-)	_____
19. be(s)t	bet	(+)(-)	_____
20. li(f)t	lit	(+)(-)	_____

Diagnostic Assessment

Sound Substitution

This phonemic awareness test assesses a child's ability to manipulate sounds in words. Read each word aloud. Ask the child to replace the target sound with the sound provided. Allow the child to use letter cards to form each word. Record the child's response on the blank. Circle each correct response. Then tally the total number correct. A score of 4 or higher on each subtest indicates proficiency with the skill.

Initial Sound Substitution

"Listen to the word I say. Then replace the first sound with the sound I say."

1. sad   Replace the first sound with /m/.   _____ (mad)
2. fish   Replace the first sound with /d/.   _____ (dish)
3. top   Replace the first sound with /h/.   _____ (hop)
4. ball   Replace the first sound with /t/.   _____ (tall)
5. light   Replace the first sound with /f/.   _____ (fight)

Score _____ /5

Final Sound Substitution

"Listen to the word I say. Then replace the last sound with the sound I say."

1. bat   Replace the last sound with /d/.   _____ (bad)
2. pig   Replace the last sound with /n/.   _____ (pin)
3. tame   Replace the last sound with /k/.   _____ (take)
4. rib   Replace the last sound with /p/.   _____ (rip)
5. fish   Replace the last sound with /t/.   _____ (fit)

Score _____ /5

Medial Sound Substitution

"Listen to the word I say. Then replace the middle sound with the sound I say."

1. road   Replace the middle sound with /ē/.   _____ (read)
2. mean   Replace the middle sound with /ā/.   _____ (main)
3. top   Replace the middle sound with /a/.   _____ (tap)
4. ball   Replace the middle sound with /e/.   _____ (bell)
5. sick   Replace the middle sound with /o/.   _____ (sock)

Score _____ /5

K–6 Diagnostic Assessment

Letter Naming and Sight Words

Letter Naming Fluency Assessment

Instructions for Administering Letter Naming Fluency

1. Place the Letter Naming Fluency record sheet in front of the student.

2. Say these specific directions to the student:

Here are some letters. Tell me the names of as many letters as you can. When I say, "Begin" start here (point to the first letter) *and go across the page. Point to each letter and tell me the name of that letter. If you come to a letter that you don't know, I'll tell it to you. Put your finger on the first letter. Ready, begin.*

3. Start your stopwatch. Follow along with the Letter Naming Fluency record sheet. Put a (/) through letters named incorrectly. Place a check above letters named correctly.

4. At the end of 1 minute, place a bracket (]) after the last letter named and say, *Stop.*

Directions for Scoring

1. If the student does not get any correct letter names within the first 10 letters (1 row), discontinue the task and record a score of zero.

2. If the student hesitates for 3 seconds on a letter, score the letter incorrect, and provide the correct letter to the student.

3. If the student provides the letter sound rather than the letter name, say: *Remember to tell me the letter name, not the sound it makes.* If the student continues providing letter sounds, mark each letter as incorrect, and make a note of this behavior at the bottom of the page.

4. Score a point for each correct letter the student names and record the total number of correct letters at the bottom of the sheet.

5. See the **Letter Naming Fluency Growth Table** on page 76 to obtain a letter naming fluency score.

Letter Naming and Sight Words Grades K-2

Name _____ Date _____

Letter Naming Fluency										# correct
g	a	t	X	r	F	C	j	T	z	__ /10
K	l	q	z	b	n	y	s	I	O	__ /10
A	e	V	u	Q	Y	Z	M	j	a	__ /10
f	i	W	R	g	U	d	z	S	c	__ /10
k	M	g	D	o	J	n	p	m	h	__ /10
C	N	E	b	u	a	g	w	V	f	__ /10
G	Y	i	d	e	n	S	T	t	c	__ /10
R	F	a	m	Z	I	w	v	C	n	__ /10
f	s	P	o	T	W	E	j	k	Q	__ /10
D	U	g	e	A	b	i	y	B	d	__ /10
N	f	p	R	F	q	l	K	p	M	__ /10
L	a	W	f	U	c	O	b	x	Z	__ /10

Total ___ /120

Sight Word Fluency Assessment

Instructions for Administering the Assessment

Give the student the assessment sheet, and have the student put his or her finger on the first word in the first row. Explain that you would like the student to read as many words as he or she can in one minute. Tell the student to point to each word and say the word. Then say: *When you are ready, you may begin.* Start your stopwatch, timing the student for one minute as he or she reads the words.

1. Follow along as the student reads. Place a check above each word that is said correctly.

2. Place a line through each word that is read incorrectly or omitted.

3. If the student substitutes or mispronounces a word, put a line through the word and write the word the student said above it.

4. If the student does not correctly say a word within 3 seconds, say the word for the student and mark the word as incorrect.

5. Say *Stop* at the end of one minute and place a bracket (]) after the last word read by the student.

Directions for Scoring

1. Count the total number of words read. This includes the words that are read correctly and incorrectly. Record that number on the table at the bottom of the sheet.

2. Count the number of errors for each line of words in the # of errors column. Record the total number of errors in the bottom table.

3. Use this formula to score Oral Reading Accuracy:

$$\frac{\text{Total No. of Words Read} - \text{No. of Errors}}{\text{Total Number of Words Read}} \times 100$$

Name _____ Date _____

Sight Word Fluency					# of errors
and	are	do	for	go	(5)
has	have	he	here	is	(5)
like	little	look	me	my	(5)
play	said	see	she	to	(5)
the	this	was	we	what	(5)
where	with	you	jump	not	(5)
up	too	yes	over	run	(5)
come	good	on	that	very	(5)
help	use	now	could	one	(5)
two	they	her	does	who	(5)
some	of	at	live	into	(5)
many	out	want	under	show	(5)

Total number of words read in one minute	
Number of errors	
Accuracy rate (use Oral Reading Accuracy formula)	

Letter Naming and Sight Words Grades K-2

AIMSweb® Growth Table
Letter Naming Fluency
Multi-year Aggregate

Grade	%ile	Fall Num	Fall LNC	Winter Num	Winter LNC	Spring Num	Spring LNC	ROI
K	90		37		55		65	0.8
	75		25		45		54	0.8
	50		11		33		42	0.9
	25	13377	3	12037	20	12653	31	0.8
	10		0		8		19	0.5
	Mean		15		33		42	0.8
	StdDev		15		17		18	
1	90		65		76		79	0.4
	75		55		66		69	0.4
	50		44		55		58	0.4
	25	10887	32	2518	44	1455	47	0.4
	10		22		32		36	0.4
	Mean		44		55		58	0.4
	StdDev		17		17		17	

Num = Number of Students   **LNC** = Letter Names Correct   **ROI** = Rate Of Improvement
ROI is Spring Score minus Fall Score (or Winter minus Fall) divided by 36 weeks (or 18 weeks)

AIMSweb® Growth Table
Phoneme Segmentation Fluency
Multi-year Aggregate

Grade	%ile	Fall Num	Fall PC	Winter Num	Winter PC	Spring Num	Spring PC	ROI
K	90		44		48		62	0.5
	75		32		34		51	0.5
	50		14		14		37	0.6
	25	1870	3	13234	5	14103	15	0.3
	10		0		0		5	0.1
	Mean		19		20		35	0.4
	StdDev		17		19		22	
1	90		56		62		67	0.3
	75		46		54		59	0.4
	50		33		43		50	0.5
	25	13615	15	10197	31	8269	39	0.7
	10		6		16		26	0.6
	Mean		31		42		48	0.5
	StdDev		19		18		16	

Num = Number of Students   **PC** = Phonemes Correct   **ROI** = Rate Of Improvement
ROI is Spring Score minus Fall Score (or Winter minus Fall) divided by 36 weeks (or 18 weeks)

Diagnostic Assessment

K–6 Diagnostic Assessment

Phonics and Decoding

- **Hasbrouck's Phonics Survey**

Phonics Survey, Standard Version

Jan Hasbrouck, Ph.D.
© 2005 JH Consulting

*The purpose of the Phonics Survey (PS)
is to provide informal diagnostic information that can be used
to help (a) PLAN a student's instructional program in basic word
reading skills, and (b) MONITOR THE PROGRESS or
IMPROVEMENT in phonics skill development. The PS has
not been normed or standardized. It is meant to be used as
an informal classroom assessment tool.*

Directions for Administration and Scoring

1. Say to the student:

   "I'm going to ask you to read some letters, words, and sentences to me so I can find out what kinds of words are easy for you to read and what kinds of words you still need to learn. I want you to try to do your best. We probably won't do this whole page; we'll stop if it gets too hard. Do you have any questions?"

   Start the PS assessment where you believe the student's skills are fairly strong. For beginning readers (K–1 level), start with sounds or letter names.

   For the *NAMES* task, have the student name the letter Q, not the *qu* digraph. For the *SOUNDS* task, have the student give you the short sound for each of the vowels. If the student says the long sound (letter name), say: *"That is one sound that letter makes. Do you know the <u>short</u> sound for that letter?"* For the letter *c*, ask for the "hard sound" /k/, as in *cat*. For the letter *g* ask for the "hard sound" /g/, as in *gas*. For the letter *y* ask for the /y/ sound, as in *yes*. If the student offers a correct alternative sound for these letters, you should say, *"Yes, that is one sound for that letter. Do you know another sound that letter makes?"*

   Most students in 4th grade and above would not be given the letter names/sounds task. Letter names would usually only be given to K–1st students. (If a student reads 6/10 or more in Task 2a, you may skip Task 1 Letter Sounds.)

2. If the student has difficulty (half or fewer correct on any task) move up the page to an easier task. If the student does well (more than half correct on a task), move down to a harder task.

3. On Tasks 2–6: If the student reads all or almost all words correctly on part (a) of the task (reading words), you may want to skip part (b) of the task (reading sentences). If the next task is difficult for the student, you can go back and complete the part of a previous task that was skipped.

4. When the student is reading the words in text, only count errors on the target words (those underlined and in italics).

5. Stop the assessment when the student appears frustrated or tired. It is OK to stop in the middle of a task. Not all tasks must be administered, but try to assess as many as possible so you will have sufficient information to plan instruction or monitor progress.

6. Mark errors and make notes or comments to help you remember how the student responded. Note that in Task 9, students read the entire word, not syllable- by -syllable. The teacher's copy is written in syllables to facilitate marking/recording of errors within a word.

7. The PS is scored by each individual task *only*. Record the ratio of correct responses over the total number possible, (e.g., 13/21 or 8/10 for each task). A chart format can be helpful for reporting PS results.

1. Letters		Score
(a) Names	N/A not administered	_____ /26
(b) Sounds		18 /21 cons.
		4 /5 vowels
2. VC and CVC		Score
(a) List		8 /10
(b) Text		17 /20
3. Digraphs		Score
(a) List		6 /10
(b) Text		4 /10

8. The grade level listed above each task is an approximate level at which those phonics skills are often taught. **NOTE**: *Results from the PS CAN ONLY be used to determine a student's strengths/needs in key phonics and decoding skills, NOT his or her grade-level performance in reading.*

Phonics and Decoding Grades K-6

Phonics Survey—Standard Version

Task 1(a)	m t a s i r d f o
	g l h u c n b j k
Task 1(b)	y e w p v qu x z

Task 2(a)	wat fod leb tum pon
	sib cug raf mip hev
Task 2(b)	Sam and Ben hid the gum. Pat had a nap in bed. Mom had a top on a big pot. Tim can sit in a tub.

Task 3(a)	shap ming gack whum pith
	chan thog kosh mich whaf
Task 3(b)	That duck had a wet wing. Brad hit a log with a whip. When can Chip pack? A fish is in that tub.

Task 4(a)	clab trin snaf greb slad
	fosp lonk mant jast sund
Task 4(b)	Glen will swim past the raft in the pond. The frog must flip and spin and jump.

Task 5(a)	sice nole fune moze vate
	rine lade sile gane fote
Task 5(b)	Mike and Jane use a rope to ride the mule. Pete had five tapes at home.

Phonics Survey—Standard Version

Task 6(a)	cort pirk varb serl surd tarn forp murk tirn kerm
Task 6(b)	The tar on his torn shirt burned and hurt him. The bird hid under the short ferns in the park.
Task 7(a)	litch mudge glux quam celp gerb knaz gnap wrill ralk
Task 7(b)	The cider is in the wrong cup. She ran to the center of the bridge. I will stitch a knot on the quilt. The giant can gnaw on the box.
Task 8	foat roast frea creak moom scoop raim waist folt scold dray gray chout mount poid join moy royal vaul fault praw straw koe toe frew jewel palk scald pigh fight
Task 9(a)	mascot basket moment bacon handle puzzle cartoon order escape chowder
Task 9(b)	amputate liberty dominate elastic entertain practical innocent electric volcano segregate
Task 9(c)	particular contaminate community superior vitality evaporate inventory prehistoric solitary emergency
Task 10	discount dismiss nonsense nostop index intent prefix prepare return regard unable uncertain confident concert station motion famous joyous madness witness portable drinkable fastest dampest mouthful fearful honorary literary instrument fragment

Phonics and Decoding Grades K–6

Grades K–1														
1. Letters						Score		**(b) Sounds**						Score
(a) Names	m	t	a	s	i	r		/m/	/t/	/a/	/s/	/i/	/r/	
	d	f	o	g	l	h		/d/	/f/	/o/	/g/	/l/	/h/	/21 cons.
	u	c	n	b	j	k		/u/	/k/	/n/	/b/	/j/	/k/	
	y	e	w	p	v	qu		/y/	/e/	/w/	/p/	/v/	/kw/	
	x	z					/26	/ks/	/z/					/5 vowels

Grade 1				
2. VC and CVC		Comments		Score
(a) In List	wat fod leb tum pon sib cug raf mip hev			/10
(b) In Text	*Sam* and *Ben* *hid* the *gum*. *Pat* *had* a *nap* *in* *bed*. *Mom* *had* a *top* *on* a *big* *pot*. *Tim* *can* *sit* *in* a *tub*.			/20

Grade 1				
3. Consonant Digraphs		Comments		Score
(a) In List	shap ming gack whum pith chan thog kosh mich whaf			/10
(b) In Text	*That* *duck* had a wet *wing*. *Brad* hit a log *with* a *whip*. *When* can *Chip* *pack*? A *fish* is in *that* tub.			/10

Grade 1				
4. CVCC and CCVC		Comments		Score
(a) In List	clab trin snaf greb slad fosp lonk mant jast sund			/10
(b) In Text	*Glen* will *swim* *past* the *raft* in the *pond*. The *frog* *must* *flip* and *spin* and *jump*.			/10

Grades 1–2				
5. Silent e		Comments		Score
(a) In List	sice nole fune moze vate rine lade sile gane fote			/10
(b) In Text	*Mike* and *Jane* *use* a *rope* to *ride* the *mule*. *Pete* had *five* *tapes* at *home*.			/10

Phonics and Decoding Grades K–6

Grades 1–2

6. r-Controlled Vowels

					Comments	Score
(a) In List	cort	pirk	varb	serl		
	surd	tarn	forp	murk		
	tirn	kerm				/10
(b) In Text	The *tar* on his *torn* *shirt* *burned* and *hurt* him.					
	The *bird* hid *under* the *short* *ferns* in the *park*.					/10

Grades 1–3

7. Advanced Consonants (–tch, -dge, -x, qu, soft c & g, kn, gn, wr, -lk)

					Comments	Score
(a) In List	litch	mudge	glux	quam		
	celp	gerb	knaz	gnap		
	wrill	ralk				/10
(b) In Text	The *cider* is in the *wrong* cup.	She ran to the *center* of the *bridge*.				
	I will *stitch* a *knot* on the *quilt*.	The *giant* can *gnaw* on the *box*.				/10

Grades 1–3

8. Vowel Teams

oa, ea, oo, ai, ol, ay, ou, oi, oy, au, aw, oe, ew, al, igh							Comments	Score
foat	roast	frea	creak	moom	scoop	raim		
waist	folt	scold	dray	gray	chout			
mount	poid	join	moy	royal	vaul	fault		
praw	straw	koe	toe	frew	jewel	palk		
scald	pigh	fight						/30

Grades 2, 3, 4–6+

9. Multi-Syllable

					Comments	Score
(a) 2-Syllable	mas-cot	bas-ket	mo-ment	ba-con		
	han-dle	puz -zle	car-toon	or-der		
	es-cape	chow-der				/10
(b) 3-Syllable	am-pu-tate	lib-er-ty	dom-in-ate	e-las-tic		
	en-ter-tain	prac-ti-cal	in-no-cent	e-lec-tric		
	vol-ca-no	seg-re-gate				/10
(c) 4-Syllable	par-tic-u-lar	con-tam-in-ate	com-mu-ni-ty	su-per-i-or		
	vi-tal-i-ty	e-vap-or-ate	in-ven-tor-y	pre-his-tor-ic		
	sol-i-tar-y	e-mer-gen-cy				/10

Grades 2, 3, 4–6+

10. Prefixes and Suffixes

dis-, non-, in-, pre-, re-, un-, con-, -tion, -ous, -ness, -able, -est, -ful, -ary, -ment					Comments	Score
discount	dismiss	nonsense	nonstop	index		
intent	prefix	prepare	return	regard		
unable	uncertain	confident	concert	station		
motion	famous	joyous	madness	witness		
portable	drinkable	fastest	dampest	mouthful		
fearful	honorary	literary	instrument	fragment		/30

Diagnostic Assessment

Oral Reading Fluency

- **Fluency Passages for Grades K–6**
- **National Fluency Norms**

Introduction

What Is Fluency?

Fluency is the critical bridge between two key elements of reading—decoding and comprehension. In its 2000 report, the National Reading Panel defined it as "the ability to read text quickly, accurately, and with proper expression." Fluency has several dimensions. Successful readers must decode words accurately. But they must move beyond decoding and recognize words in connected text quickly and automatically. They must also read with expression in order to bring meaningful interpretation to the text. All three dimensions— accurate decoding, automaticity, and ability to read expressively—work together to create effective comprehension and overall success in reading.

In its 1994 study of reading, the National Assessment of Educational Progress (NAEP) established a clear connection between fluency and comprehension. NAEP defined fluency as the ease or "naturalness" of reading. It recognized certain key elements as contributing to fluency. These included the reader's grouping or phrasing of words as shown through intonation, stress, and pauses and the reader's adherence to the author's syntax. They also included expressiveness as reflected by the reader's interjection of a sense of feeling, anticipation, or characterization in oral reading. These elements are called *prosody*. When readers use appropriate volume, tone, emphasis, and phrasing, they give evidence of comprehension. They demonstrate that they are actively constructing meaning from the text.

Why Is Fluency Important?

Fluency is critical because it directly impacts the comprehension process. For years, teachers thought that if students could decode words accurately, they would become strong readers. Fluency, which has been referred to as a "neglected" aspect of reading, received little attention. Now it is recognized as one of the five critical components of reading.

Researchers have pointed out that people can successfully focus on only one thing at a time. They can, however, do more than one thing at a time if one of those things is so well learned that it can be done automatically. In its simplest form, reading can be seen as (1) word identification or decoding and (2) comprehension, or the active construction of meaning. Effective readers cannot focus on both of these processes at the same time. If a reader is focused almost entirely on decoding, that reader will have few resources left over for constructing meaning. Only when readers can read the words in connected text automatically are they free to focus their attention on making inferences, drawing conclusions, and applying other critical thinking skills associated with constructing meaning.

A fluent reader generally reads with speed and accuracy, but in addition usually displays these kinds of behaviors:

- Recognizes words automatically

- Applies graphophonic, semantic, and syntactic cues to recognize unfamiliar words

- Segments texts into meaningful chunks
- Emulates the sounds and rhythms of spoken language while reading aloud

A nonfluent reader, in contrast, may display these kinds of behaviors:

- Reads slowly and laboriously
- Processes text word-by-word in a choppy manner
- Frequently ignores punctuation
- Fails to use meaningful phrasing
- Shows little certainty when reading high-frequency words

Fluency does not mean only rapid reading. Occasionally, you will come across a nonfluent reader who is able to read text rapidly but fails to use appropriate phrasing. This reader often ignores meaning and punctuation. As a result, this reader struggles to answer questions about what has been read and fails to grasp the intent of the text.

Why Assess Fluency?

Students need to be fluent in order to be proficient readers. Their oral reading fluency can be improved through explicit training, but you need to assess their fluency level before you can determine what specific fluency-building activities and materials will be appropriate. In addition, students excel in reading when they are given opportunities to read as much connected text as possible at their independent level. Fluency assessment helps you determine what this level is.

The oral reading fluency assessments in this book answer this question: *How many words can a student read aloud per minute and how many of these words are read correctly?* This book also helps you observe reading performance beyond speed and accuracy by providing a rubric similar to the one developed by NAEP. This 4-level rubric on page 4 takes into account additional aspects of fluency, such as prosody.

How and When to Assess

Kindergarten Through Early First Grade

Until children can decode and automatically recognize many words by sight, they cannot be expected to read aloud effortlessly and expressively. That is why formally assessing their oral reading fluency at this early stage is not recommended. However, it is highly recommended that kindergarten children be involved in fluency-building activities, such as listening to books being read aloud and imitating auditory models of natural speech. Toward the end of kindergarten, children can be given opportunities to reread familiar, predictable, and decodable text to build fluency.

Some assessments for children at these grade levels are considered valuable. By assessing letter naming, phoneme segmentation, and sight word fluency during kindergarten and the early part of Grade 1, teachers can determine what type of fluency-building activities and materials to provide. Assessments for these skill areas appear in other sections of this book.

Midyear of Grade 1 Through Grade 6

Curriculum-based assessment of oral reading fluency is administered by asking a student to do a timed reading of a carefully selected on-level passage. As the student reads, you follow along in a copy of the same text and record errors such as omissions, substitutions, misreadings, insertions of words or parts of words, and hesitations of more than three seconds. Self-corrections and repetitions are not considered errors. To calculate the number of words read correctly in one minute, subtract the number of errors from the total number of words read. This process should be repeated periodically throughout the school year to monitor growth.

The Fluency Passages

The fluency passages serve two purposes. They can be administered three times a year as benchmark tests to determine if students are on track. They can also be used every unit so that you can monitor progress and determine if students are meeting instructional goals.

Oral Fluency Scale

Prosody Rubric

Level 4
- The student: reads in large, meaningful phrases; may occasionally repeat words or short phrases, but the overall structure and syntax of the passage is not affected; reads at an appropriate rate of speed with expressive interpretation.

Level 3
- The student: reads in three- and four-word phrases; reads primarily in phrases that preserve the passage's syntax and structure; attempts to read expressively; generally reads at an appropriate rate of speed.

Level 2
- The student: reads mainly in two-word phrases, with some longer phrases and at times word-by-word; may group words awkwardly and not connect phrases to the larger context of the passage; reads sections of the passage excessively slowly or quickly.

Level 1
- The student: reads word-by-word, with some longer phrases; does not phrase meaningfully or with an appropriate rate of speed; reads the passage excessively slowly.

Oral Reading Fluency Grades 1–6

Curriculum-Based Oral Reading Fluency Norms

Use these norms to interpret your students' oral reading fluency abilities and to tailor instruction to their individual needs. Results are based on a one-minute timed sampling of students reading aloud. A more detailed chart appears on pages 102–103.

Grade	Percentile	Fall WCPM	Winter WCPM	Spring WCPM
1	90	NA	81	111
	75	NA	47	82
	50	NA	23	53
	25	NA	12	28
	10	NA	6	15
	SD	NA	32	39
2	90	106	125	142
	75	79	100	117
	50	51	72	89
	25	25	42	61
	10	11	18	31
	SD	37	41	42
3	90	128	146	162
	75	99	120	137
	50	71	92	107
	25	44	62	78
	10	21	36	48
	SD	40	43	44
4	90	145	166	180
	75	119	139	152
	50	94	112	123
	25	68	87	98
	10	45	61	72
	SD	40	41	43
5	90	166	182	194
	75	139	156	168
	50	110	127	139
	25	85	99	109
	10	61	74	83
	SD	45	44	45
6	90	177	195	204
	75	153	167	177
	50	127	140	150
	25	98	111	122
	10	68	82	93
	SD	42	45	44
7	90	180	192	202
	75	156	165	177
	50	128	138	150
	25	102	109	123
	10	79	88	98
	SD	40	43	41
8	90	185	193	199
	75	161	173	177
	50	133	146	151
	25	106	115	124
	10	77	84	97
	SD	43	45	41

> A student's scores should fall within a range of ten WCPM above or below the score shown.

KEY
WCPM: Words correct per minute
SD: Average standard deviation of scores

SOURCE Hasbrouck, J. & Tindal, G. (2005) norms for oral reading fluency. Eugene, OR: Behavioral Research & Teaching, University of Oregon.

Oral Reading Fluency Grades 1–6

Administering Fluency Assessments and Using the Fluency Record

Directions

Give a student a reading passage he or she has not seen before. Fluency assessments are always done as "cold reads"; that is, they are done with material that is new to the person being tested. Explain that you would like the student to read the passage out loud and then answer two questions about it. Then say: *When you are ready, you may begin.* Start your stopwatch when the student reads the first word.

1. Follow along on your copy of the passage as the student reads. Place a line through each word that is read incorrectly or omitted.

2. Place a check above each word that is read correctly.

3. If the student substitutes or mispronounces a word, put a line through the word and write the word the student said above it.

4. If the student does not correctly say the word within 3 seconds, say the word for the student and circle the word to mark it as incorrect. Self-corrections and repetitions are not marked as errors.

5. At the end of one minute, stop your stopwatch and place a bracket (]) after the last word read by the student.

6. Have the student finish reading the passage.

7. Read the comprehension questions to the student. Have the student answer the comprehension questions orally.

How to Score

Record the information for each student on the fluency record sheet for that passage.

1. Look at the number in the left margin of the passage, on the same line as the bracket. (Note: In hyphenated words, individual words are counted as one word.) Add to this number all the words before the bracket to figure out how many words the student was able to read in one minute.

2. Count each word you circled or put a line through. The total is the number of errors made. Subtract this number from the number of words read in one minute to arrive at the Oral Reading Fluency Rate, or Words Correct Per Minute score.

3. Use this formula to score Oral Reading Accuracy:

$$\frac{\text{Total No. of Words Read} - \text{No. of Errors}}{\text{Total Number of Words Read}} \times 100$$

An Oral Reading Accuracy Scoring Chart is also provided on the inside of the back cover to help you calculate the percentage.

Diagnostic Assessment

Oral Reading Fluency Grades 1-6

4. On the Prosody Rubric, circle 1, 2, 3, or 4 depending on your evaluation of the student's performance. A score of 4 is the highest possible score.

5. Write comments about oral reading performance on the sheet, including the student's ability to answer the comprehension questions.

Scoring Sample

The Oral Fluency Record Sheet is an assessment tool to help you record oral reading accuracy and important aspects of oral reading fluency. Information gathered from the fluency record sheet may be used to verify or clarify instructional decisions.

Oral Reading Accuracy is a percentage score based on the total number of words read and the number of errors noted. The student should read 97% or more of the words correctly. A scoring chart for measuring Oral Reading Accuracy is provided on the inside back cover for your convenience.

Oral Reading Fluency is a score that is equivalent to the total number of words read in one minute minus the number of errors made.

Oral Fluency Record Sheet

Name_____ Date _____

Oral Reading Accuracy: _____%

Oral Reading Fluency Score: _____ words correct per minute

Prosody Rubric: (Circle Score) 1 2 3 4

Circle: Fall Winter Spring

The Prosody Rubric is a rubric for evaluating oral reading performance. It groups observable behaviors into levels.

Comprehension Question Responses

#1 _____

#2 _____

Scoring Sample

Jane and Dean were best pals. They rode their bikes to

11 school (together.) At recess, they always played on the same

21 team. Jane and Dean like to race home at school and do their

34 homework together. Then Pepper came along. Pepper was Jane's

43 new black puppy. Dean felt bad because Jane spent all her time with

56 Pepper now. Dean missed his best friend. One day, Dean sat on his

69 (front) steps alone. He closed his eyes and thought about all the fun

82 he and Jane used to have. Suddenly,] something licked his face and

94 Dean opened his eyes. Jane and Pepper had come to play. Now Dean

107 had two best pals. 111

No. of words read corrrectly: 86/111

No. of errors made: 3/111

The Bug

I see a bug. It has six legs.
It is red. It is very small.
It is fun to look at it.
The bug is very busy.
I see it go up a hill.
I see it come down.
I see it dig. I see it stop.
The sun is out now. It is a hot sun.
It is time for a nap.
The bug naps in the sun.
I will nap in the sun, too.

1. What is this story mostly about?

2. Why does the bug take a nap?

Diagnostic Assessment

Oral Fluency Record Sheet

Name _____ Date _____

Oral Reading Accuracy: _____%   Circle: Fall   Winter   Spring

Oral Reading Fluency Score: _____ words correct per minute

Prosody Rubric: (Circle Score) 1 2 3 4

Comprehension Question Responses

#1 _____

#2 _____

The Bug

	I see a bug. It has six legs.
8	It is red. It is very small.
15	It is fun to look at it.
22	The bug is very busy.
27	I see it go up a hill.
34	I see it come down.
39	I see it dig. I see it stop.
47	The sun is out now. It is a hot sun.
57	It is time for a nap.
63	The bug naps in the sun.
69	I will nap in the sun, too. **76**

Number of words read: _____   Number of errors made: _____

© Macmillan/McGraw-Hill

Ben's Birthday

Today is Ben's birthday.
I am helping Mom make a cake.
We mix eggs and milk.
Then Mom adds more good things.
The batter is thick and white.
Mom puts the batter into a pan.
She puts the pan into the oven.
"I think Ben will like his cake," I say.
Time passes. Then I think I smell smoke.
Is it the cake? Mom runs in. But the cake is fine.
Now we are ready for Ben's birthday.
Dad picks Ben up to see his cake.
Ben smiles and claps his hands.
"You are one year old today!" we all say.

1. What is the story about?

2. Why couldn't Ben bake the cake?

Oral Fluency Record Sheet

Name _____ Date _____

Oral Reading Accuracy: _____%   Circle: Fall   Winter   Spring
Oral Reading Fluency Score: _____ words correct per minute
Prosody Rubric: (Circle Score) 1 2 3 4
Comprehension Question Responses
#1 _____
#2 _____

Ben's Birthday

	Today is Ben's birthday.
4	I am helping Mom make a cake.
11	We mix eggs and milk.
16	Then Mom adds more good things.
22	The batter is thick and white.
28	Mom puts the batter into a pan.
35	She puts the pan into the oven.
42	"I think Ben will like his cake," I say.
51	Time passes. Then I think I smell smoke.
59	Is it the cake? Mom runs in. But the cake is fine.
71	Now we are ready for Ben's birthday.
78	Dad picks Ben up to see his cake.
86	Ben smiles and claps his hands.
92	"You are one year old today!" we all say. 101

Number of words read: _____   **Number of errors made:** _____

You and Your Shadow

Do you like to play with your shadow?
You can use your hands to make pictures on a wall.
You can make animal heads and funny shapes.
Light makes the shadows.
Light might hit you on one side.
Your shadow would fall on the other side.
When you are outside, sunlight makes shadows.
The sun may make long shadows or short ones.
In the morning and evening, the sun is low.
Shadows are long.
At noon, the sun is high. Shadows are short.
Is your shadow in front of you?
Then the light is behind you.
Is your shadow behind you?
Then the light is in front of you.
You are never alone. You always have your shadow.

1. What makes shadows?

2. What would your shadow look like in the morning?

Oral Fluency Record Sheet

Name _____ Date _____

Oral Reading Accuracy: _____%   Circle: Fall   Winter   Spring

Oral Reading Fluency Score: _____ words correct per minute

Prosody Rubric: (Circle Score) 1 2 3 4

Comprehension Question Responses

#1 _____

#2 _____

You and Your Shadow

	Do you like to play with your shadow?
8	You can use your hands to make pictures on a wall.
19	You can make animal heads and funny shapes.
27	Light makes the shadows.
31	Light might hit you on one side.
38	Your shadow would fall on the other side.
46	When you are outside, sunlight makes shadows.
53	The sun may make long shadows or short ones.
62	In the morning and evening, the sun is low.
71	Shadows are long.
74	At noon, the sun is high. Shadows are short.
83	Is your shadow in front of you?
90	Then the light is behind you.
96	Is your shadow behind you?
101	Then the light is in front of you.
109	You are never alone. You always have your shadow. **118**

Number of words read: _____   **Number of errors made:** _____

Our American Flag

Our flag is special to us.
It stands for our country. It is red, white, and blue.
The flag has 13 stripes. It has 50 stars.
There were 13 states when our country was born.
There are 50 states in our country now.
We call our flag the Stars and Stripes.
That is what we see when we look at the flag.
Here are some rules about the flag.
Fly the flag outside in good weather.
Take the flag down at night.
Take the flag inside when it rains.
Never let the flag touch the ground.
Follow these rules.
They show that you are proud of your flag.

1. What does each star stand for on the flag?

2. How can you care for your flag?

Oral Fluency Record Sheet

Name _____ Date _____

Oral Reading Accuracy: _____%   Circle: Fall   Winter   Spring
Oral Reading Fluency Score: _____ words correct per minute
Prosody Rubric: (Circle Score) 1 2 3 4
Comprehension Question Responses
#1 _____
#2 _____

Our American Flag

	Our flag is special to us.
6	It stands for our country. It is red, white, and blue.
17	The flag has 13 stripes. It has 50 stars.
26	There were 13 states when our country was born.
35	There are 50 states in our country now.
43	We call our flag the Stars and Stripes.
51	That is what we see when we look at the flag.
62	Here are some rules about the flag.
70	Fly the flag outside in good weather.
77	Take the flag down at night.
83	Take the flag inside when it rains.
90	Never let the flag touch the ground.
97	Follow these rules.
100	They show that you are proud of your flag. 109

Number of words read: _____   **Number of errors made:** _____

The New Friend

Jane and Dean were best pals. They rode their bikes to school together every day. They were both in Mrs. Green's class. At recess, they always played on the same baseball team. Jane and Dean liked to race home after school and do their homework together.

Then Pepper came along. Pepper was Jane's new black puppy. Dean felt sad because Jane spent all her time with Pepper now. Dean missed his best friend.

One day, Dean sat on his front steps alone. He closed his eyes and thought about all the fun he and Jane used to have.

Suddenly, something licked his face, and Dean opened his eyes. Jane and Pepper had come to play. Now Dean had two best pals.

1. Why was Dean sad?

2. Why do you think Jane and Pepper came to play?

Oral Fluency Record Sheet

Name _____ Date _____

Oral Reading Accuracy: _____%   Circle: Fall   Winter   Spring

Oral Reading Fluency Score: _____ words correct per minute

Prosody Rubric: (Circle Score) 1 2 3 4

Comprehension Question Responses

#1 _____

#2 _____

The New Friend

	Jane and Dean were best pals. They rode their
9	bikes to school together every day. They were both
18	in Mrs. Green's class. At recess, they always
26	played on the same baseball team. Jane and Dean
35	liked to race home after school and do their
44	homework together.
46	Then Pepper came along. Pepper was Jane's
53	new black puppy. Dean felt sad because Jane
61	spent all her time with Pepper now. Dean missed
70	his best friend.
73	One day, Dean sat on his front steps alone. He
83	closed his eyes and thought about all the fun he
93	and Jane used to have.
98	Suddenly, something licked his face, and Dean
105	opened his eyes. Jane and Pepper had come to
114	play. Now Dean had two best pals. 121

© Macmillan/McGraw-Hill

Number of words read: _____   **Number of errors made:** _____

Sharks

Sharks have lived on Earth for years and years. Today there are more than 350 different kinds. Sharks come in many sizes. The whale shark can be 36 feet in length. The smallest shark grows only to about 6 inches. Some sharks have big, sharp teeth. Others have very small teeth. But all sharks have one thing in common. They all must open their mouths to breathe. Sharks must keep their mouths open when they swim, or they will die.

Every year sharks are killed for many reasons. They get caught in fishing nets. Some are caught to be sold for shark meat or shark fin soup. Shark skin is sometimes used for belts. Other people hunt them because they think sharks are dangerous. Will sharks be around much longer?

1. How does a shark breathe?
2. Why are sharks in danger?

Oral Fluency Record Sheet

Name _____ Date _____

Oral Reading Accuracy: _____%   Circle: Fall   Winter   Spring

Oral Reading Fluency Score: _____ words correct per minute

Prosody Rubric: (Circle Score) 1 2 3 4

Comprehension Question Responses

#1 _____

#2 _____

Sharks

	Sharks have lived on Earth for years and years.
9	Today there are more than 350 different kinds. Sharks
18	come in many sizes. The whale shark can be 36
28	feet in length. The smallest shark grows only to about
38	6 inches. Some sharks have big, sharp teeth.
46	Others have very small teeth. But all sharks have one
56	thing in common. They all must open their mouths to
66	breathe. Sharks must keep their mouths open when
74	they swim, or they will die.
80	Every year sharks are killed for many
87	reasons. They get caught in fishing nets. Some
95	are caught to be sold for shark meat or shark fin
106	soup. Shark skin is sometimes used for belts.
114	Other people hunt them because they think
121	sharks are dangerous. Will sharks be around
128	much longer? 130

Number of words read: _____   Number of errors made: _____

Fun for Marge

Marge the cat did not feel like chasing mice today. She wanted some fun for a change. Marge strolled across the street and into a schoolyard. She wanted to watch what the children were doing there.

Marge slid through the door and hid in a cardboard box. Not long after that, someone picked up the box. Marge swayed as she was carried through a narrow hall. Then the swaying stopped.

In a flash, Marge was out of the box. She could not believe her eyes. All the children were running and chasing balls. Marge thought they were all pretending to be cats, and joined in the game.

Soon the children were chasing Marge, but she did not like this kind of fun. Marge ran down the hall and out the door. After that day, Marge thought chasing mice was just enough fun for a feline.

1. Why did Marge go to the schoolyard?

2. Why would Marge think the children were pretending to be cats?

Oral Fluency Record Sheet

Name _____ Date _____

Oral Reading Accuracy: _____%   Circle: Fall   Winter   Spring
Oral Reading Fluency Score: _____ words correct per minute
Prosody Rubric: (Circle Score) 1 2 3 4
Comprehension Question Responses
#1 _____
#2 _____

Fun for Marge

	Marge the cat did not feel like chasing mice
9	today. She wanted some fun for a change. Marge
18	strolled across the street and into a schoolyard.
26	She wanted to watch what the children were
34	doing there.
36	Marge slid through the door and hid in a
45	cardboard box. Not long after that, someone picked
53	up the box. Marge swayed as she was carried
62	through a narrow hall. Then the swaying stopped.
70	In a flash, Marge was out of the box. She could
81	not believe her eyes. All the children were running and
91	chasing balls. Marge thought they were all pretending
99	to be cats, and joined in the game.
107	Soon the children were chasing Marge,
113	but she did not like this kind of fun. Marge ran
124	down the hall and out the door. After that day,
134	Marge thought chasing mice was just enough
141	fun for a feline. 145

Number of words read: _____   Number of errors made: _____

The White House

The White House is the home of the President of the United States. It is indeed a big, white house. A painter would need 570 gallons of white paint to cover all the outside walls!

The White House has 6 floors, 132 rooms, and 32 bathrooms. Some rooms are for the President's family and friends. Other rooms are used as offices or for meetings. Parties and other celebrations are held in some rooms. The biggest room is the East Room. It is used for balls and parties. The President has small dinners in the Blue Room. Big dinners, on the other hand, take place in the State Dining Room.

You would enjoy a visit to the White House. The tour takes you to five of the rooms. You might even meet the President!

---

1. What is this story about?

2. Tell what three of the rooms in the White House are used for.

Oral Fluency Record Sheet

Name _____ Date _____

Oral Reading Accuracy: _____%   Circle: Fall   Winter   Spring

Oral Reading Fluency Score: _____ words correct per minute

Prosody Rubric: (Circle Score) 1 2 3 4

Comprehension Question Responses

#1 _____

#2 _____

The White House

	The White House is the home of the President
9	of the United States. It is indeed a big, white house.
20	A painter would need 570 gallons of white paint to
30	cover all the outside walls!
35	The White House has 6 floors, 132 rooms,
43	and 32 bathrooms. Some rooms are for the
51	President's family and friends. Other rooms are
58	used as offices or for meetings. Parties and other
67	celebrations are held in some rooms. The biggest
75	room is the East Room. It is used for balls and
86	parties. The President has small dinners in the
94	Blue Room. Big dinners, on the other hand, take
103	place in the State Dining Room.
109	You would enjoy a visit to the White House.
118	The tour takes you to five of the rooms. You might
129	even meet the President! 133

Number of words read: _____   **Number of errors made:** _____

A Birthday Party

Molly turned eight on Sunday. She did not expect a party because she knew her mom had millions of other things to do. But that morning her mom told Molly that they should take a walk in the park. When they got there, Molly saw her closest friends. Five girls and three boys all shouted, "Happy birthday!" Molly was really surprised. Her mom had planned everything. There were snacks. There were games to play. There was even a cake with eight candles.

After eating yummy snacks, the friends played games. Jack won a prize for making a funny face. Kate won a balloon for blowing the biggest bubble. Grace won marbles for hopping on one foot. Everyone got stickers just because they took part in a game.

Then the kids sang to Molly. She blew out the candles and everyone ate cake. Molly was so happy. She thanked all her friends for making her birthday special. She hugged and kissed her mom for giving her the best birthday ever.

1. Name two things that Molly did at her birthday party.

2. Why did Molly's mom suggest that they walk in the park?

Diagnostic Assessment

Oral Fluency Record Sheet

Name _____   Date _____

Oral Reading Accuracy: _____%   Circle: Fall Winter Spring
Oral Reading Fluency Score: _____ words correct per minute
Prosody Rubric: (Circle Score) 1 2 3 4
Comprehension Question Responses
#1 _____
#2 _____

A Birthday Party

	Molly turned eight on Sunday. She did not expect
9	a party because she knew her mom had millions of other
20	things to do. But that morning her mom told Molly that
31	they should take a walk in the park. When they got there,
43	Molly saw her closest friends. Five girls and three boys
53	all shouted, "Happy birthday!" Molly was really
60	surprised. Her mom had planned everything. There
67	were snacks. There were games to play. There was
76	even a cake with eight candles.
82	After eating yummy snacks, the friends
88	played games. Jack won a prize for making a funny
98	face. Kate won a balloon for blowing the biggest
107	bubble. Grace won marbles for hopping on one foot.
116	Everyone got stickers just because they took part
124	in a game.
127	Then the kids sang to Molly. She blew out the
137	candles and everyone ate cake. Molly was so
145	happy. She thanked all her friends for making her
154	birthday special. She hugged and kissed her
161	mom for giving her the best birthday ever. **169**

© Macmillan/McGraw-Hill

Number of words read: _____   **Number of errors made:** _____

Fossils

Dinosaurs lived on Earth millions of years ago. Today we know a lot about them. How do we know so much? We learned about them from people who study the remains of dead plants and animals.

Fossils is the name we give to remains that have become hard and turned to stone. Not every plant or animal becomes a fossil when it dies. Some just dry up under the sun. Strong winds blow away others.

For a dead plant or animal to become a fossil, everything must be just right. Sand or mud has to cover the animal or plant quickly. That way, neither the wind nor the sun can destroy it. Then the sand or mud cover turns hard as a rock. Over time, the fossil takes shape.

To find fossils, we must dig for them. We might find a bone, a tooth, or part of a plant. We might even find a footprint! Every find is a clue that tells a little more about life many years ago.

1. How do people find fossils?

2. Why are the sun and the wind a problem when creating new fossils?

Oral Fluency Record Sheet

Name _____ Date _____

Oral Reading Accuracy: _____%   Circle: Fall   Winter   Spring

Oral Reading Fluency Score: _____ words correct per minute

Prosody Rubric: (Circle Score) 1 2 3 4

Comprehension Question Responses

#1 _____

#2 _____

Fossils

7	Dinosaurs lived on Earth millions of years ago. Today we know a lot about them. How do we
18	know so much? We learned about them from people
27	who study the remains of dead plants and animals.
36	Fossils is the name we give to remains that
45	have become hard and turned to stone. Not every
54	plant or animal becomes a fossil when it dies.
63	Some just dry up under the sun. Strong winds blow
73	away others.
75	For a dead plant or animal to become a fossil,
85	everything must be just right. Sand or mud has to
95	cover the animal or plant quickly. That way, neither
104	the wind nor the sun can destroy it. Then the sand or
116	mud cover turns hard as a rock. Over time, the fossil
127	takes shape.
129	To find fossils, we must dig for them. We might
139	find a bone, a tooth, or part of a plant. We might even
152	find a footprint! Every find is a clue that tells a little
164	more about life many years ago. **170**

Number of words read: _____   **Number of errors made:** _____

Basketball on Wheels

Basketball is a challenging sport to play. Players need strength to move up and down the court and bounce the ball while they are on the move. They also need to be alert for the opportunity to pass. Basketball players cannot relax or let their attention stray for a second. People who play basketball work as a team and depend on each other for support. The same is true for people who play basketball from wheelchairs.

The United States has many basketball teams for children in wheelchairs. The children on these teams bounce the ball, pass, and shoot from their wheelchairs. They learn to move quickly in their chairs and keep track of the ball. They must also be good at passing and shooting. They need a lot of balance, energy, and upper-body strength. Just think how high the basketball hoop looks when you are sitting down.

Wheelchair basketball is an excellent way for children in wheelchairs to be on a team. These players show us we can all be strong if we make the effort.

1. Name three things that are needed by all kinds of basketball players.

2. Why is it important for children in wheelchairs to get the chance to play basketball?

Oral Fluency Record Sheet

Name _____ Date _____

Oral Reading Accuracy: _____%   Circle: Fall   Winter   Spring

Oral Reading Fluency Score: _____ words correct per minute

Prosody Rubric: (Circle Score) 1 2 3 4

Comprehension Question Responses

#1 _____

#2 _____

Basketball on Wheels

	Basketball is a challenging sport to play. Players need
9	strength to move up and down the court and bounce the ball while
22	they are on the move. They also need to be alert for the opportunity
36	to pass. Basketball players cannot relax or let their attention stray
47	for a second. People who play basketball work as a team and
59	depend on each other for support. The same is true for people who
72	play basketball from wheelchairs.
76	The United States has many basketball teams for
84	children in wheelchairs. The children on these teams bounce
93	the ball, pass, and shoot from their wheelchairs. They learn to
104	move quickly in their chairs and keep track of the ball. They
116	must also be good at passing and shooting. They need a lot of
129	balance, energy, and upper-body strength. Just think how
138	high the basketball hoop looks when you are sitting down.
148	Wheelchair basketball is an excellent way for children
156	in wheelchairs to be on a team. These players show us we can
169	all be strong if we make the effort. 177

Number of words read: _____   Number of errors made: _____

The Pet Rock

Emma still has the pet rock she received for her birthday five years ago. It is still one of her favorite possessions. It is gray with fuzzy orange feet and a lavender tail. Its eyes are outlined in blue and white crayon, and its mouth is drawn in red crayon.

Rob brought the pet rock to Emma's birthday party when she turned six. It was wrapped in a huge yellow box with an enormous bright red bow. When Emma opened the box, she found another box inside wrapped in sparkly green paper. Inside that box was another box wrapped in pink tissue paper. Finally, inside that box was her pet rock.

It was the best gift Emma got that year and the only one she still has from her sixth birthday. It was special and different because Rob had made it himself.

Emma keeps it on a shelf in her room next to the trophy she won at last year's swim competition. When Emma looks at the rock, she remembers Rob, her party that year, and what friendship really means. It is still one of her best memories.

1. Why was Rob's gift so special and different?
2. What was unusual about the way the pet rock was wrapped?

Oral Fluency Record Sheet

Name _____ Date _____

Oral Reading Accuracy: _____%   Circle: Fall   Winter   Spring
Oral Reading Fluency Score: _____ words correct per minute
Prosody Rubric: (Circle Score) 1 2 3 4
Comprehension Question Responses
#1 _____
#2 _____

The Pet Rock

	Emma still has the pet rock she received for her
10	birthday five years ago. It is still one of her favorite
21	possessions. It is gray with fuzzy orange feet and a
31	lavender tail. Its eyes are outlined in blue and white crayon,
42	and its mouth is drawn in red crayon.
50	Rob brought the pet rock to Emma's birthday party
59	when she turned six. It was wrapped in a huge yellow box
71	with an enormous bright red bow. When Emma opened the
81	box, she found another box inside wrapped in sparkly green
91	paper. Inside that box was another box wrapped in pink
101	tissue paper. Finally, inside that box was her pet rock.
111	It was the best gift Emma got that year and the only
123	one she still has from her sixth birthday. It was special and
135	different because Rob had made it himself.
142	Emma keeps it on a shelf in her room next to the
154	trophy she won at last year's swim competition. When
163	Emma looks at the rock, she remembers Rob, her party that
174	year, and what friendship really means. It is still one of
185	her best memories. 188

Number of words read: _____   **Number of errors made:** _____

The Giant Panda

The giant panda is an animal with a chubby, black-and-white body and black legs. Its head is large and round, and its white face has black patches around each eye.

Panda cubs are extremely tiny when they are born, weighing only about five ounces. As adults, however, giant pandas can weigh as much as 350 pounds.

Giant pandas live only in places where there are bamboo forests with plenty of bamboo shoots for them to eat. Because of this, they are found only on high mountain slopes in western and southwestern China. Giant pandas can spend 16 hours a day eating. In one year, a panda can eat more than 10,000 pounds of bamboo. Although the giant panda eats chiefly bamboo shoots, it sometimes eats other plants, fish, and small animals, too.

As a special gift to the people of the United States, China gave two giant pandas to the National Zoo in Washington, D.C., in 1972. The pandas lived there for many years, eating bamboo shoots and making all of the zoo visitors laugh.

1. Where do giant pandas live?
2. Why were the giant pandas from China a good gift?

Diagnostic Assessment

Oral Fluency Record Sheet

Name _____   Date _____

Oral Reading Accuracy: _____%   Circle: Fall Winter Spring
Oral Reading Fluency Score: _____ words correct per minute
Prosody Rubric: (Circle Score) 1 2 3 4
Comprehension Question Responses
#1 _____
#2 _____

The Giant Panda

	The giant panda is an animal with a chubby, black-
10	and-white body and black legs. Its head is large and round,
22	and its white face has black patches around each eye.
32	Panda cubs are extremely tiny when they are born,
41	weighing only about five ounces. As adults, however, giant
50	pandas can weigh as much as 350 pounds.
58	Giant pandas live only in places where there are
67	bamboo forests with plenty of bamboo shoots for them to eat.
78	Because of this, they are found only on high mountain
88	slopes in western and southwestern China. Giant pandas
96	can spend 16 hours a day eating. In one year, a panda can
109	eat more than 10,000 pounds of bamboo. Although the
118	giant panda eats chiefly bamboo shoots, it sometimes eats
127	other plants, fish, and small animals, too.
134	As a special gift to the people of the United States,
145	China gave two giant pandas to the National Zoo in
155	Washington, D.C., in 1972. The pandas lived there for many
165	years, eating bamboo shoots and making all of the zoo
175	visitors laugh. 177

Number of words read: _____   Number of errors made: _____

© Macmillan/McGraw-Hill

One Birthday for All

Every family has traditions. Traditions are things people do year after year. Beth King's family has many traditions they celebrate, but Beth's favorite tradition is about birthdays.

Because Beth has so many aunts, uncles, and cousins, it is impossible to celebrate each birthday. So once a year, on the third Saturday in July, Beth's relatives have one big birthday celebration for everyone. The adults stay at Beth's grandparents' house. The children sleep in tents on the lawn.

Everyone brings food and every meal is a feast. The cousins play soccer. Grandpa and the uncles sit on the wide porch and drink homemade lemonade. The aunts have a softball game. Everyone roots for their favorite team.

Afterward, everyone eats hamburgers and fresh corn. At the end, Grandma brings out a big frosted cake.

Every year, after the family birthday celebration, Beth goes to bed and starts thinking about next year's birthday party.

1. What is Beth's favorite family tradition?
2. Why does the family have their birthday celebration in the summer?

© Macmillan/McGraw-Hill

Oral Fluency Record Sheet

Name _____ Date _____

Oral Reading Accuracy: _____%   Circle: Fall   Winter   Spring
Oral Reading Fluency Score: _____ words correct per minute
Prosody Rubric: (Circle Score) 1 2 3 4
Comprehension Question Responses
#1 _____
#2 _____

One Birthday for All

	Every family has traditions. Traditions are things
7	people do year after year. Beth King's family has many
17	traditions they celebrate, but Beth's favorite tradition is
25	about birthdays.
27	Because Beth has so many aunts, uncles, and
35	cousins, it is impossible to celebrate each birthday.
43	So once a year, on the third Saturday in July, Beth's
54	relatives have one big birthday celebration for everyone.
62	The adults stay at Beth's grandparents' house. The
70	children sleep in tents on the lawn.
77	Everyone brings food and every meal is a feast.
86	The cousins play soccer. Grandpa and the uncles sit
95	on the wide porch and drink homemade lemonade.
103	The aunts have a softball game. Everyone roots for their
113	favorite team.
115	Afterward, everyone eats hamburgers and fresh
121	corn. At the end, Grandma brings out a big frosted cake.
132	Every year, after the family birthday celebration,
139	Beth goes to bed and starts thinking about next year's
149	birthday party. 151

Number of words read: _____   **Number of errors made:** _____

© Macmillan/McGraw-Hill

Ruiz's Toy Chest

Ruiz is almost nine, and he has decided that he has outgrown his old toys. He goes to his toy chest and empties out all his old playthings. His wooden helicopter, some coloring books, his stuffed giraffe, his parrot puppet, and all his other old toys are spread around him on the floor.

"I'll bet the little kid next door would really enjoy playing with some of this stuff," Ruiz thinks to himself as he looks at all of his old toys.

Ruiz picks up his stuffed giraffe with its black nose, orange stripes, long neck, and funny feet. He remembers how he used to pretend he was on the grassy plains of Africa riding on his giraffe.

"Maybe I'll keep my giraffe after all," thinks Ruiz, and he puts the giraffe back into the toy chest.

Ruiz peers into the toy chest. "My giraffe looks really lonely in there," he thinks. "I'd better put the other toys back in so that he'll have some more company."

Ruiz collects all the other toys and puts them back into the toy chest. "I think I'll keep all these old friends a little bit longer," he says to himself.

1. Why does Ruiz plan to give away his old toys?
2. Why does Ruiz decide to keep his old giraffe?

Oral Fluency Record Sheet

Name _____ Date _____

Oral Reading Accuracy: _____%   Circle: Fall   Winter   Spring

Oral Reading Fluency Score: _____ words correct per minute

Prosody Rubric: (Circle Score) 1 2 3 4

Comprehension Question Responses

#1 _____

#2 _____

Ruiz's Toy Chest

	Ruiz is almost nine, and he has decided that he
10	has outgrown his old toys. He goes to his toy chest
21	and empties out all his old playthings. His wooden
30	helicopter, some coloring books, his stuffed giraffe,
37	his parrot puppet, and all his other old toys are spread
48	around him on the floor.
53	"I'll bet the little kid next door would really
62	enjoy playing with some of this stuff," Ruiz thinks to
72	himself as he looks at all of his old toys.
82	Ruiz picks up his stuffed giraffe with its black
91	nose, orange stripes, long neck, and funny feet. He
100	remembers how he used to pretend he was on the
110	grassy plains of Africa riding on his giraffe.
118	"Maybe I'll keep my giraffe after all," thinks
126	Ruiz, and he puts the giraffe back into the toy chest.
137	Ruiz peers into the toy chest. "My giraffe
145	looks really lonely in there," he thinks. "I'd better put
155	the other toys back in so that he'll have some
165	more company."
167	Ruiz collects all the other toys and puts them
176	back into the toy chest. "I think I'll keep all these old
188	friends a little bit longer," he says to himself. 197

Number of words read: _____   **Number of errors made:** _____

Bill Peet, Writer and Artist

Bill Peet is a popular children's writer and artist. Many of his books have animal characters because he loved to draw animals. The animals act like people and were often like people Bill Peet knew.

Before he began writing children's books, Bill Peet wrote and drew illustrations for the movies. He worked on famous films like *Peter Pan* and *Sleeping Beauty*.

Many of Bill Peet's books are very funny, but at the same time they talk about serious problems. In his book *Farewell to Shady Glade*, a group of animals has to leave its home because people want to put up buildings where they live. The animals lose their home, and the reader doesn't know if they will find a new one.

Other books give lessons about life. The book *Kermit the Hermit* is about a selfish crab. After a boy rescues him, Kermit learns that it is important to share.

Through Bill Peet's books, both children and adults get to see the world through new eyes. They get to laugh, but at the same time they get to learn important lessons about life.

1. Who is Bill Peet?
2. Why is Bill Peet an important writer?

© Macmillan/McGraw-Hill

Oral Fluency Record Sheet

Name _____ Date _____

Oral Reading Accuracy: _____%   **Circle:** Fall   Winter   Spring

Oral Reading Fluency Score: _____ words correct per minute

Prosody Rubric: (Circle Score) 1 2 3 4

Comprehension Question Responses

#1 _____

#2 _____

Bill Peet, Writer and Artist

	Bill Peet is a popular children's writer and
8	artist. Many of his books have animal characters
16	because he loved to draw animals. The animals act like
26	people and were often like people Bill Peet knew.
35	Before he began writing children's books, Bill Peet
43	wrote and drew illustrations for the movies. He worked
52	on famous films like *Peter Pan* and *Sleeping Beauty.*
61	Many of Bill Peet's books are very funny, but at
71	the same time they talk about serious problems. In his
81	book *Farewell to Shady Glade,* a group of animals has to
92	leave its home because people want to put up buildings
102	where they live. The animals lose their home, and the
112	reader doesn't know if they will find a new one.
122	Other books give lessons about life. The book
130	*Kermit the Hermit* is about a selfish crab. After a boy
141	rescues him, Kermit learns that it is important
149	to share.
151	Through Bill Peet's books, both children and
158	adults get to see the world through new eyes. They get to
170	laugh, but at the same time they get to learn important
181	lessons about life. **184**

© Macmillan/McGraw-Hill

Number of words read: _____   **Number of errors made:** _____

Deep Sleep

Making it through the winter is hard for many animals. Some animals and insects, like birds and butterflies, are able to migrate to warmer places. Other animals, such as bears, cannot make such a far move.

To survive the icy weather, many bears go to sleep. This sleep is called hibernation. Preparing for this deep sleep keeps bears busy throughout late summer and fall. During this time, they must eat a lot of berries and fish. The food helps them gain at least 40 pounds a week. They must store enough body fat because they have to live off this fat while asleep.

For its long sleep, a bear finds a cave or hollow log. Its heart rate may drop from 40 to 10 beats a minute. Most bears start hibernating in early October. When they wake up around April or May, they are very hungry. Be very careful if you know there are bears near where you are living. You would not want to be in the path of a hungry bear.

1. Why do bears sleep during the winter?
2. Why are bears especially dangerous in the spring?

Diagnostic Assessment

Oral Fluency Record Sheet

Name _____ Date _____

Oral Reading Accuracy: _____%   **Circle: Fall Winter Spring**
Oral Reading Fluency Score: _____ words correct per minute
Prosody Rubric: (Circle Score) 1 2 3 4
Comprehension Question Responses
#1 _____
#2 _____

Deep Sleep

	Making it through the winter is hard for many animals. Some
11	animals and insects, like birds and butterflies, are able to migrate to
23	warmer places. Other animals, such as bears, cannot make such a
34	far move.
36	To survive the icy weather, many bears go to sleep. This sleep
48	is called hibernation. Preparing for this deep sleep keeps bears busy
59	throughout late summer and fall. During this time, they must eat a lot
72	of berries and fish. The food helps them gain at least 40 pounds a
86	week. They must store enough body fat because they have to live off
99	this fat while asleep.
103	For its long sleep, a bear finds a cave or hollow log. Its heart
117	rate may drop from 40 to 10 beats a minute. Most bears start
130	hibernating in early October. When they wake up around April or
141	May, they are very hungry. Be very careful if you know there are bears
155	near where you are living. You would not want to be in the path
169	of a hungry bear. 173

© Macmillan/McGraw-Hill

Number of words read: _____   **Number of errors made:** _____

How Skunk Got His Stripes

Skunk did not always have white stripes. Long ago, he was all black. He was black from the tip of his nose to the end of his tail. At night, this was a big problem for the other animals. They could not see Skunk coming.

"We have to solve this problem!" said Bobcat. Skunk had sprayed him just the night before with his scent.

"It is not my fault," said Skunk. "You animals come crashing through my home in the middle of the night. You scare me half to death. What do you expect me to do?"

"I have an idea," said Fawn shyly. Everyone turned to the youngster in surprise. "Perhaps we should give Skunk white spots like mine. Then we could see him in the dark."

Even Skunk thought this was a fine solution. So Bobcat borrowed a bucket of white paint from a farmer's barn. Squirrel said he would paint spots on Skunk.

Squirrel started painting Skunk's back. But then he came to Skunk's tail. He saw that his tail was too bushy for polka dots. The animals decided that stripes would work just as well. And to this day, all skunks have striped tails.

1. What problem were the animals trying to solve?
2. What was Squirrel's solution?

Diagnostic Assessment

Oral Fluency Record Sheet

Name _____   Date _____

Oral Reading Accuracy: _____%   Circle: Fall   Winter   Spring

Oral Reading Fluency Score: _____ words correct per minute

Prosody Rubric: (Circle Score) 1 2 3 4

Comprehension Question Responses

#1 _____

#2 _____

How Skunk Got His Stripes

	Skunk did not always have white stripes. Long ago, he
10	was all black. He was black from the tip of his nose to the end
25	of his tail. At night, this was a big problem for the other
38	animals. They could not see Skunk coming.
45	"We have to solve this problem!" said Bobcat. Skunk
54	had sprayed him just the night before with his scent.
64	"It is not my fault," said Skunk. "You animals come
74	crashing through my home in the middle of the night. You
85	scare me half to death. What do you expect me to do?"
97	"I have an idea," said Fawn shyly. Everyone turned to
107	the youngster in surprise. "Perhaps we should give Skunk
116	white spots like mine. Then we could see him in the dark."
128	Even Skunk thought this was a fine solution. So Bobcat
138	borrowed a bucket of white paint from a farmer's barn.
148	Squirrel said he would paint spots on Skunk.
156	Squirrel started painting Skunk's back. But then he
164	came to Skunk's tail. He saw that his tail was too bushy for
177	polka dots. The animals decided that stripes would work just as
188	well. And to this day, all skunks have striped tails. **198**

Number of words read: _____   **Number of errors made:** _____

© Macmillan/McGraw-Hill

Play Ball

What do baseball players need? To start with, they need a bat and ball. A baseball bat is long and round. Most bats are made of ash wood. The bat cannot be longer than 46 inches. It cannot be thicker than $2\frac{3}{4}$ inches at any point. A baseball is small, hard, and round. It weighs about 5 ounces. It has a tiny cork ball at the center. Layers of rubber and yarn are tightly wrapped around this ball. The cover of the ball is made of two pieces of white cowhide. These are sewn together with thick red thread.

Next, players need a special padded leather glove. They also need shoes with spikes on the soles. The spikes help them stop and start quickly.

At bat, players wear a batting helmet. This is a special hard cap. The helmet protects batters in case they are hit in the head with the ball.

In baseball, a pitcher pitches the ball to a catcher. Catchers have special equipment to protect them. They wear a metal mask over their faces. They also wear padded cloth covers over their chests. To protect their legs, they wear hard shin guards.

Baseball can be safe and fun. Are you ready to play ball?

1. What is a baseball made of?
2. Why do baseball players wear special clothing?

Diagnostic Assessment

Oral Fluency Record Sheet

Name _____ Date _____

Oral Reading Accuracy: _____%   Circle: Fall   Winter   Spring

Oral Reading Fluency Score: _____ words correct per minute

Prosody Rubric: (Circle Score) 1 2 3 4

Comprehension Question Responses

#1 _____

#2 _____

Play Ball

	What do baseball players need? To start with, they need a
11	bat and a ball. A baseball bat is long and round. Most bats are
25	made of ash wood. The bat cannot be longer than 46 inches. It
38	cannot be thicker than $2\frac{3}{4}$ inches at any point. A baseball is
50	small, hard, and round. It weighs about 5 ounces. It has a tiny cork
64	ball at the center. Layers of rubber and yarn are tightly wrapped
76	around this ball. The cover of the ball is made of two pieces of
90	white cowhide. These are sewn together with thick red thread.
100	Next, players need a special padded leather glove. They also
110	need shoes with spikes on the soles. The spikes help them stop and
123	start quickly.
125	At bat, players wear a batting helmet. This is a special hard
137	cap. The helmet protects batters in case they are hit in the head
150	with the ball.
153	In baseball, a pitcher pitches the ball to a catcher. Catchers
164	have special equipment to protect them. They wear a metal mask
175	over their faces. They also wear padded cloth covers over their
186	chests. To protect their legs, they wear hard shin guards.
196	Baseball can be safe and fun. Are you ready to play ball? **208**

© Macmillan/McGraw-Hill

Number of words read: _____   **Number of errors made:** _____

Climbing the Walls

Jill's dad loved rock climbing. He took many trips to the mountains. He wanted Jill to come with him. But first Jill had to learn about climbing.

Jill was excited. She and her dad found a climbing wall in town. Jill put on a helmet and climbing shoes. Then she put on ropes and other gear. Jill's ropes were fastened to the floor. From there, they went around her dad's waist. Then, they went up to the top of the wall.

"I will hold the rope tight," her dad said. "You will be safe. Just go slowly."

Jill looked up at the wall. She saw places for her hands and feet. The top looked far away.

Jill started up. She went from spot to spot. She reached out with her hands. She pushed hard with her feet. At last, she was near the top.

"I can't climb this last bit," she called down.

"Just try," her dad called back. "I'm holding you."

Jill took hold of something small with her hand. She bent down. Then she jumped. Her hand felt the top of the wall. She pulled herself up. She had made it.

"Will you ever do that again?" asked her dad after Jill got back down.

"Oh, yes!" said Jill. "That was great!"

---

1. What is this story mostly about?
2. Do you think Jill felt safe the whole time she was climbing? Why?

Diagnostic Assessment

Oral Fluency Record Sheet

Name _____ Date _____

Oral Reading Accuracy: _____%   **Circle: Fall Winter Spring**

Oral Reading Fluency Score: _____ **words correct per minute**

Prosody Rubric: (Circle Score) 1 2 3 4

Comprehension Question Responses

#1 _____

#2 _____

Climbing the Walls

	Jill's dad loved rock climbing. He took many trips to the
11	mountains. He wanted Jill to come with him. But first Jill had to
24	learn about climbing.
27	Jill was excited. She and her dad found a climbing wall in
39	town. Jill put on a helmet and climbing shoes. Then she put on
52	ropes and other gear. Jill's ropes were fastened to the floor. From
64	there, they went around her dad's waist. Then, they went up to the
77	top of the wall.
81	"I will hold the rope tight," her dad said. "You will be safe.
94	Just go slowly."
97	Jill looked up at the wall. She saw places for her hands and
110	feet. The top looked far away.
116	Jill started up. She went from spot to spot. She reached out
128	with her hands. She pushed hard with her feet. At last, she was
141	near the top.
144	"I can't climb this last bit," she called down.
153	"Just try," her dad called back. "I'm holding you."
162	Jill took hold of something small with her hand. She bent
173	down. Then she jumped. Her hand felt the top of the wall. She
186	pulled herself up. She had made it.
193	"Will you ever do that again?" asked her dad after Jill got
205	back down.
207	"Oh, yes!" said Jill. "That was great!" **214**

Number of words read: _____   **Number of errors made:** _____

Up, Up, and Away

For thousands of years, people dreamed of flying. They tried many things. Nothing seemed to work.

Then in 1783, two brothers in France got a new idea. They were watching smoke. They noticed the way smoke moves up from a fire. It does not seem to come back down. The brothers filled paper bags with smoke. They watched as the smoke moved the bags into the air.

The brothers decided to make a big balloon. They filled it with smoke. When it was full, they let it go. Up, up it went.

Next, the brothers built another balloon. This time they attached a basket to the balloon. In September 1783, they were ready. They put a rooster, a duck, and a sheep in the basket. They filled the balloon with hot air and let it go. Up it went, this time with passengers. Then, high above the Earth, the warm air cooled. The balloon floated back to the ground. The three animals had taken a round-trip air flight.

Two other Frenchmen watched these events. They decided to become the first people to fly. They built a big blue and gold balloon. In November 1783, the balloon carried them over the city of Paris.

Today we take air travel for granted. But not too long ago, flight was still a mystery and a challenge.

1. What is this passage mainly about?
2. Explain what makes the balloons rise.

Oral Reading Fluency Grades 1–6

Oral Fluency Record Sheet

Name _____ Date _____

Oral Reading Accuracy: _____%   Circle: Fall   Winter   Spring

Oral Reading Fluency Score: _____ words correct per minute

Prosody Rubric: (Circle Score) 1 2 3 4

Comprehension Question Responses

#1 _____

#2 _____

Up, Up, and Away

	For thousands of years, people dreamed of flying. They
9	tried many things. Nothing seemed to work.
16	Then in 1783, two brothers in France got a new idea. They
28	were watching smoke. They noticed the way smoke moves up
38	from a fire. It does not seem to come back down. The brothers
51	filled paper bags with smoke. They watched as the smoke moved
62	the bags into the air.
67	The brothers decided to make a big balloon. They filled it
78	with smoke. When it was full, they let it go. Up, up it went.
92	Next, the brothers built another balloon. This time they
101	attached a basket to the balloon. In September 1783, they were
112	ready. They put a rooster, a duck, and a sheep in the basket. They
126	filled the balloon with hot air and let it go. Up it went, this time
141	with passengers. Then, high above the Earth, the warm air cooled.
152	The balloon floated back to the ground. The three animals had
163	taken a round-trip air flight.
169	Two other Frenchmen watched these events. They decided
177	to become the first people to fly. They built a big blue and gold
191	balloon. In November 1783, the balloon carried them over the city
202	of Paris.
204	Today we take air travel for granted. But not too long ago,
216	flight was still a mystery and a challenge. **224**

Number of words read: _____   Number of errors made: _____

The Great Wall of China

One of the wonders of the world stands in China. It is the Great Wall of China. The Great Wall is the longest structure ever built. It is about 4,600 miles long.

The Chinese built the wall as protection against enemies. It was started more than 2,500 years ago. Workers made big piles of dirt. They pounded the dirt until it was very hard. They would use this hard dirt to build the wall. Over time the wall crumbled. It was rebuilt again and again.

Often, the wall did not work. For example, in the 1200s, enemies climbed over it to conquer China.

Today, people see the wall that went up between 1368 and 1644. This wall went up during the Ming Dynasty. At first, the Ming built the old way. They piled and pounded dirt. But rain and wind destroyed these walls. The builders turned to stone and brick. These walls took longer to build. They cost more, too. But they lasted longer.

The new wall had towers. Soldiers lived in some of them. They sent signals from others. For signals, they built fires. They used smoke during the day. At night they used flames. People far away could get ready for an attack.

Today, the wall is crumbling. No one knows how much longer it will stand. Rain and wind break parts of the wall. Some people take bricks. Others write on the wall. The wall once protected China. Now China must protect the wall.

1. What is special about the Great Wall of China?
2. Why was the Great Wall built?

Oral Fluency Record Sheet

Name _____ Date _____

Oral Reading Accuracy: _____%   Circle: Fall   Winter   Spring

Oral Reading Fluency Score: _____ words correct per minute

Prosody Rubric: (Circle Score) 1 2 3 4

Comprehension Question Responses

#1 _____

#2 _____

The Great Wall of China

	One of the wonders of the world stands in China. It is the
13	Great Wall of China. The Great Wall is the longest structure ever
25	built. It is about 4,600 miles long.
32	The Chinese built the wall as protection against enemies. It
42	was started more than 2,500 years ago. Workers made big piles of
54	dirt. They pounded the dirt until it was very hard. They would
66	use this hard dirt to build the wall. Over time the wall crumbled.
79	It was rebuilt again and again.
85	Often, the wall did not work. For example, in the 1200s,
96	enemies climbed over it to conquer China.
103	Today, people see the wall that went up between 1368
113	and 1644. This wall went up during the Ming Dynasty. At
124	first, the Ming built the old way. They piled and pounded dirt. But
137	rain and wind destroyed these walls. The builders turned to stone
148	and brick. These walls took longer to build. They cost more, too.
160	But they lasted longer.
164	The new wall had towers. Soldiers lived in some of them.
175	They sent signals from others. For signals, they built fires. They
186	used smoke during the day. At night they used flames. People far
198	away could get ready for an attack.
205	Today, the wall is crumbling. No one knows how much
215	longer it will stand. Rain and wind break parts of the wall. Some
228	people take bricks. Others write on the wall. The wall once
239	protected China. Now China must protect the wall. **247**

Number of words read: _____   Number of errors made: _____

The Little Brother

Anna thought her little brother was a real pest. He sat on her bed while she gossiped on the telephone. He watched her as she did her homework. He sat on the floor at her feet as she watched TV. Matt was three years old. Anna knew he loved her. She loved him, too, but enough was enough.

One afternoon, Anna was sitting at her tiny desk in the corner of the family room. She was trying to finish her math homework. Matt kept asking her questions about the spiral notebook she was using. He also wanted to know about the numbers that she was writing. And why, he asked, did she use her eraser so often? Finally, Anna pleaded with her mother for some help. She just wanted some peace and quiet.

Anna's mother smiled. Then she asked Anna if she would like it if her friends always shooed her away. Anna suddenly saw that Matt was her friend, as well as her brother. She gave him a crayon and a piece of notebook paper. Then she made room for him at her desk.

1. What did Anna's little brother do to annoy her?
2. How did Anna's mother help her see her brother differently?

Oral Fluency Record Sheet

Name _____ Date _____

Oral Reading Accuracy: _____%   Circle: Fall   Winter   Spring

Oral Reading Fluency Score: _____ words correct per minute

Prosody Rubric: (Circle Score) 1 2 3 4

Comprehension Question Responses

#1 _____

#2 _____

The Little Brother

	Anna thought her little brother was a real pest. He sat on
12	her bed while she gossiped on the telephone. He watched her as
24	she did her homework. He sat on the floor at her feet as she
38	watched TV. Matt was three years old. Anna knew he loved her.
50	She loved him, too, but enough was enough.
58	One afternoon, Anna was sitting at her tiny desk in the
69	corner of the family room. She was trying to finish her math
81	homework. Matt kept asking her questions about the spiral
90	notebook she was using. He also wanted to know about the
101	numbers that she was writing. And why, he asked, did she use
113	her eraser so often? Finally, Anna pleaded with her mother for
124	some help. She just wanted some peace and quiet.
133	Anna's mother smiled. Then she asked Anna if she would
143	like it if her friends always shooed her away. Anna suddenly saw
155	that Matt was her friend, as well as her brother. She gave him a
169	crayon and a piece of notebook paper. Then she made room for
181	him at her desk. 185

© Macmillan/McGraw-Hill

Number of words read: _____   **Number of errors made:** _____

Moons

Many years ago, Native Americans did not have calendars to tell them what month or day it was. Instead, they had the moon. By keeping track of the time it took for the moon to go from one full moon phase to the next, they measured their days.

Each phase was called a moon, and each moon was about the length of a month. They noted how cold the winds were and what the Earth looked like around them. They observed what color the rabbits' fur was, and if choke cherries were on the bushes. Then they named that moon phase for what they saw and felt.

March might be the Moon of the Long Rains to a Native American living in the Northeast. To a Native American in a dry climate, March might be the Moon of the Desert Blooms. Moons could also be named after feasts and ceremonies, such as the moon of Summer Encampment. Children learned about the moons from their elders, and looked forward to what each new moon would bring.

1. How did Native Americans keep track of what month or day it was?

2. How did Native Americans decide what to name a moon phase?

Diagnostic Assessment

Oral Fluency Record Sheet

Name _____ Date _____

Oral Reading Accuracy: _____%   Circle: Fall   Winter   Spring

Oral Reading Fluency Score: _____ words correct per minute

Prosody Rubric: (Circle Score) 1 2 3 4

Comprehension Question Responses

#1 _____

#2 _____

Moons

	Many years ago, Native Americans did not have calendars
9	to tell them what month or day it was. Instead, they had the moon.
23	By keeping track of the time it took for the moon to go from one
38	full moon phase to the next, they measured their days.
48	Each phase was called a moon, and each moon was about the
60	length of a month. They noted how cold the winds were and what
73	the Earth looked like around them. They observed what color
83	the rabbits' fur was, and if choke cherries were on the bushes.
95	Then they named that moon phase for what they saw and felt.
107	March might be the Moon of the Long Rains to a Native
119	American living in the Northeast. To a Native American in a dry
131	climate, March might be the Moon of the Desert Blooms. Moons
142	could also be named after feasts and ceremonies, such as the
153	moon of Summer Encampment. Children learned about the moons
162	from their elders, and looked forward to what each new moon
173	would bring. 175

Number of words read: _____   Number of errors made: _____

Before and Now

You do not have to be Columbus to be interested in traveling to new places. Many people living today are just as curious as Columbus once was. These brave people leave their beloved homelands behind and move to new countries to live. These people are called *immigrants,* and they show extraordinary courage! Try to imagine leaving everything you know and love behind, and moving to a place you have never even seen before. Perhaps your parents or grandparents did just that. Maybe you are an immigrant yourself.

But what about the countries left behind? What did they look like? If you know any immigrants, ask them if they have any old photographs you can look at. What would you see in those photos? What would the automobiles look like, the buildings, even the clothes the people wore? What would these things tell you about the other place the person had lived? If you do not know anyone who has moved to this country, or you do not have any photos to look at, you can go to your local library. Look up travel books and videos. If you are extremely lucky, you may know someone who kept a diary or journal describing what life was like where he or she came from. This type of keepsake will help bring the old country and the new one together.

1. What is this passage mostly about?
2. Why might people move to a new country?

Diagnostic Assessment

Oral Fluency Record Sheet

Name _____ Date _____

Oral Reading Accuracy: _____%   **Circle: Fall Winter Spring**
Oral Reading Fluency Score: _____ words correct per minute
Prosody Rubric: (Circle Score) 1 2 3 4
Comprehension Question Responses
#1 _____
#2 _____

Before and Now

	You do not have to be Columbus to be interested
10	in traveling to new places. Many people living today are just
21	as curious as Columbus once was. These brave people leave
31	their beloved homelands behind and move to new countries
40	to live. These people are called *immigrants*, and they show
50	extraordinary courage! Try to imagine leaving everything
57	you know and love behind, and moving to a place you have
69	never even seen before. Perhaps your parents or grandparents
78	did just that. Maybe you are an immigrant yourself.
87	But what about the countries left behind? What did
96	they look like? If you know any immigrants, ask them if they
108	have any old photographs you can look at. What would you
119	see in those photos? What would the automobiles look like,
129	the buildings, even the clothes the people wore? What would
139	these things tell you about the other place the person had
150	lived? If you do not know anyone who has moved to this
162	country, or you do not have any photos to look at, you can
175	go to your local library. Look up travel books and videos.
186	If you are extremely lucky, you may know someone who
196	kept a diary or journal describing what life was like where
207	he or she came from. This type of keepsake will help bring
219	the old country and the new one together. **227**

Number of words read: _____   **Number of errors made:** _____

Why Winter Comes

Centuries ago, people noticed that Earth was warm and green some of the time and bitter cold at other times. This was a cycle that repeated itself over and over. To explain these changes, ancient people told stories. There were myths to explain just about every cycle in nature. Some stories explained why the sun disappeared each night and reappeared each morning. Other myths told what caused the moon to wax and wane.

Why winter arrived each year is explained in one myth about a Greek goddess named Demeter. The myth said that Demeter had a beautiful daughter named Persephone. Hades, the god of the underworld, snatched Persephone and brought her to his kingdom. Demeter was so depressed by her daughter's sudden disappearance that she caused Earth to become cold and barren. Nothing grew during the time that Persephone was in the underworld.

Demeter begged Hades to return her daughter. Eventually, Hades gave in and allowed the girl to return to her mother. But Demeter had to promise that Persephone would spend part of every year with him. When she saw Persephone again, Demeter was overjoyed, and she allowed plants to grow again.

This was an early explanation of why winter arrived each year. Winter was the time that Persephone had to go back to the underworld.

1. What is the author's purpose for writing this passage?
2. According to this myth, what causes winter?

© Macmillan/McGraw-Hill

Oral Reading Fluency Grades 1-6

Oral Fluency Record Sheet

Name _____ Date _____

Oral Reading Accuracy: _____%   Circle: Fall   Winter   Spring

Oral Reading Fluency Score: _____ words correct per minute

Prosody Rubric: (Circle Score) 1 2 3 4

Comprehension Question Responses

#1 _____

#2 _____

Why Winter Comes

	Centuries ago, people noticed that Earth was warm
8	and green some of the time and bitter cold at other times.
20	This was a cycle that repeated itself over and over. To explain
32	these changes, ancient people told stories. There were myths
41	to explain just about every cycle in nature. Some stories
51	explained why the sun disappeared each night and reappeared
60	each morning. Other myths told what caused the moon to
70	wax and wane.
73	Why winter arrived each year is explained in one myth about
84	a Greek goddess named Demeter. The myth said that Demeter
94	had a beautiful daughter named Persephone. Hades, the god of
104	the underworld, snatched Persephone and brought her to his
113	kingdom. Demeter was so depressed by her daughter's sudden
122	disappearance that she caused Earth to become cold and
131	barren. Nothing grew during the time that Persephone was
140	in the underworld.
143	Demeter begged Hades to return her daughter. Eventually,
151	Hades gave in and allowed the girl to return to her mother.
163	But Demeter had to promise that Persephone would spend
172	part of every year with him. When she saw Persephone again,
183	Demeter was overjoyed, and she allowed plants to grow again.
193	This was an early explanation of why winter arrived each
203	year. Winter was the time that Persephone had to go back to
215	the underworld. **217**

Number of words read: _____   Number of errors made: _____

Special Eyes

Tim and his family are raising a special puppy named Luke. Luke is a German shepherd. He was born at the guide dog center. With his three brothers and sisters, he will become a guide dog. He will learn how to help blind people.

Guide dogs help blind people cross busy streets. They help them walk inside stores and buy groceries. They help them in restaurants and on buses.

Luke's brothers and sisters are named Lark, Lisa, and Len. Why do all the names begin with the same letter? It helps the center keep track of Luke and the group.

Luke will grow up with Tim and his family. He will learn about riding in cars and living with people. When he is fourteen months old, he will go back to the center. There he will learn to obey commands. He will learn words such as "left," "right," and "sit." He will also learn to keep his mind on his work. Most dogs are distracted by sounds, smells, and other animals. Luke will learn to concentrate on leading his partner.

At Luke's graduation, Tim will meet Luke's new partner. Tim will be sad to say good-bye. But he will be happy for Luke. Luke will be a loving helper. His eyes will become special eyes for someone who needs him.

1. What is the role of Tim and his family in Luke's life?
2. What is a guide dog's job mostly about?

© Macmillan/McGraw-Hill

Oral Fluency Record Sheet

Name _____ Date _____

Oral Reading Accuracy: _____%   Circle: Fall   Winter   Spring

Oral Reading Fluency Score: _____ words correct per minute

Prosody Rubric: (Circle Score) 1 2 3 4

Comprehension Question Responses

#1 _____

#2 _____

Special Eyes

	Tim and his family are raising a special puppy named
10	Luke. Luke is a German shepherd. He was born at the guide dog
23	center. With his three brothers and sisters, he will become a
34	guide dog. He will learn how to help blind people.
44	Guide dogs help blind people cross busy streets. They
53	help them walk inside stores and buy groceries. They help them
64	in restaurants and on buses.
69	Luke's brothers and sisters are named Lark, Lisa, and Len.
79	Why do all the names begin with the same letter? It helps the
92	center keep track of Luke and the group.
100	Luke will grow up with Tim and his family. He will learn
112	about riding in cars and living with people. When he is fourteen
124	months old, he will go back to the center. There he will learn to
138	obey commands. He will learn words such as "left," "right," and
149	"sit." He will also learn to keep his mind on his work. Most dogs
163	are distracted by sounds, smells, and other animals. Luke will
173	learn to concentrate on leading his partner.
180	At Luke's graduation, Tim will meet Luke's new partner.
189	Tim will be sad to say good-bye. But he will be happy for Luke.
204	Luke will be a loving helper. His eyes will become special eyes
216	for someone who needs him. 221

Number of words read: _____   Number of errors made: _____

The Kite Contest

Jed and his little brother Tom were at the park for the kite contest. The contestant whose kite stayed up the longest would win.

The boys waited to hear their numbers. Kites swooped and soared above them. Some stayed up for a long time. Others dropped to the grass almost immediately. Finally the boys' numbers were called. Jed raced to the open field, but Tom stood still.

"I can't," he mumbled as he dropped his kite.

Jed thought for a moment. Then he went over and picked up Tom's kite. "I'll fly both of them," he said.

Jed began to run, and both kites soared into the sky. Then unexpectedly the wind jerked at Jed's kite, and the kite ripped. "My kite can't fly now," thought Jed. He dropped the string to his kite, and the kite fell to the ground. But he still had Tom's kite. He kept on running.

Suddenly the whistle blew. The contest was over. The boys met near the judge's stand to hear who had won.

"There are three winners," the judge announced. "First place goes to number 21. Second place goes to number 9. Third place goes to number 35."

"Number 35!" Jed shouted. "That's me." He jumped up and ran quickly to the judge.

"You're the one who flew two kites," the judge said. "Great job!" He handed him a green ribbon.

"It was really my brother's kite," Jed said shyly. "I'm going to share this prize with him."

---

1. What did a contestant need to do to win the contest?
2. What was unusual about the way Jed won his ribbon?

Oral Fluency Record Sheet

Name _____ Date _____

Oral Reading Accuracy: _____%   Circle: Fall   Winter   Spring
Oral Reading Fluency Score: _____ words correct per minute
Prosody Rubric: (Circle Score) 1 2 3 4
Comprehension Question Responses
#1 _____
#2 _____

The Kite Contest

	Jed and his little brother Tom were at the park for the kite
13	contest. The contestant whose kite stayed up the longest would win.
24	The boys waited to hear their numbers. Kites swooped and
34	soared above them. Some stayed up for a long time. Others dropped
46	to the grass almost immediately. Finally the boys' numbers were
56	called. Jed raced to the open field, but Tom stood still.
67	"I can't," he mumbled as he dropped his kite.
76	Jed thought for a moment. Then he went over and picked
87	up Tom's kite. "I'll fly both of them," he said.
97	Jed began to run, and both kites soared into the sky. Then
109	unexpectedly the wind jerked at Jed's kite, and the kite ripped. "My
121	kite can't fly now," thought Jed. He dropped the string to his kite,
134	and the kite fell to the ground. But he still had Tom's kite. He kept
149	on running.
151	Suddenly the whistle blew. The contest was over. The boys
161	met near the judge's stand to hear who had won.
171	"There are three winners," the judge announced. "First
179	place goes to number 21. Second place goes to number 9. Third
191	place goes to number 35."
196	"Number 35!" Jed shouted. "That's me." He
203	jumped up and ran quickly to the judge.
211	"You're the one who flew two kites," the judge said. "Great
222	job!" He handed him a green ribbon.
229	"It was really my brother's kite," Jed said shyly. "I'm going
240	to share this prize with him." **246**

Number of words read: _____   Number of errors made: _____

When You Snooze, You Lose

Carlos detested getting up in the morning. He rarely felt awake until sometime in the afternoon. By dinnertime, he was prepared for anything. By bedtime, he was unbelievably energized. Unfortunately for Carlos, school starts in the morning.

Carlos's dad resented having to wake him up ten times each morning. So his parents bought Carlos an alarm clock that had an especially loud buzz for an alarm. They informed him that getting up was now his responsibility.

The first morning, the buzz was deafening. Carlos woke up terrified. Then he realized it was simply his new alarm clock. He decided that he did not need such an earsplitting signal. Happily, he lowered the sound level.

The next morning, Carlos continued sleeping through the quiet buzz. He missed breakfast, missed the bus, and had to hustle off to school on his own two legs.

It was raining, but Carlos forgot to close his backpack. His homework got drenched and fell apart in his hands. He also forgot his lunch money as he sprinted out of the apartment. So Carlos had no lunch and then stayed after school to redo his homework. He missed the bus again and plodded home in the drizzling rain.

As soon as Carlos entered his apartment, he raced to his room and turned up the volume on his alarm. Sleeping late was just not worth it.

1. Why did Carlos's parents get him an alarm clock?

2. What lesson did Carlos learn?

© Macmillan/McGraw-Hill

Oral Fluency Record Sheet

Name _____ Date _____

Oral Reading Accuracy: _____%   Circle: Fall   Winter   Spring

Oral Reading Fluency Score: _____ words correct per minute

Prosody Rubric: (Circle Score) 1 2 3 4

Comprehension Question Responses

#1 _____

#2 _____

When You Snooze, You Lose

	Carlos detested getting up in the morning. He rarely
9	felt awake until sometime in the afternoon. By dinnertime, he was
20	prepared for anything. By bedtime, he was unbelievably energized.
29	Unfortunately for Carlos, school starts in the morning.
37	Carlos's dad resented having to wake him up ten times
47	each morning. So his parents bought Carlos an alarm clock that had
59	an especially loud buzz for an alarm. They informed him that
70	getting up was now his responsibility.
76	The first morning, the buzz was deafening. Carlos woke up
86	terrified. Then he realized it was simply his new alarm clock. He
98	decided that he did not need such an earsplitting signal. Happily, he
110	lowered the sound level.
114	The next morning, Carlos continued sleeping through the
122	quiet buzz. He missed breakfast, missed the bus, and had to hustle
134	off to school on his own two legs.
142	It was raining, but Carlos forgot to close his backpack. His
153	homework got drenched and fell apart in his hands. He also forgot
165	his lunch money as he sprinted out of the apartment. So Carlos had
178	no lunch and then stayed after school to redo his homework. He
190	missed the bus again and plodded home in the drizzling rain.
201	As soon as Carlos entered his apartment, he raced to his
212	room and turned up the volume on his alarm. Sleeping late was just
225	not worth it. **228**

Number of words read: _____   Number of errors made: _____

Mr. Lazy-Bones

Matt Kroger was incredibly lazy. He was so lazy that sometimes at dinnertime he would still be lounging in his pajamas. Putting on regular clothes was too much work, and so was tying shoes, combing hair, or striding up a one-story flight of stairs instead of taking the elevator. Matt focused on avoiding any kind of activity. But Matt loved money, so when Mrs. Tinsley asked him to walk her dog Coco, Matt grabbed the opportunity. Five dollars for a ten-minute walk was a terrific deal.

When he asked me to accompany him, I thought, "Why not? I have nothing better to do anyway."

One dog eventually led to two, because Matt discovered that walking a second pooch was like getting paid double for an identical amount of work. Then we were asked to walk a third and a fourth dog.

While strolling with the dogs, we thought, "Why not take on a paper route as well?"

"It would be like free money," Matt declared. "It won't take us any more time because we have to go around the neighborhood every day anyway."

That's right. We delivered newspapers while we walked the four dogs. Never mind that our ten-minute walk now required an investment of more than an hour. The laziest kid in the universe had become the hardest-working one of all.

1. Why did Matt decide to start walking dogs?
2. What lesson did Matt learn in this story?

Oral Fluency Record Sheet

Name _____ Date _____

Oral Reading Accuracy: _____%   Circle: Fall   Winter   Spring

Oral Reading Fluency Score: _____ words correct per minute

Prosody Rubric: (Circle Score) 1 2 3 4

Comprehension Question Responses

#1 _____

#2 _____

Mr. Lazy-Bones

	Matt Kroger was incredibly lazy. He was so lazy that
10	sometimes at dinnertime he would still be lounging in his pajamas.
21	Putting on regular clothes was too much work, and so was tying
33	shoes, combing hair, or striding up a one-story flight of stairs
45	instead of taking the elevator. Matt focused on avoiding any
55	kind of activity. But Matt loved money, so when Mrs.
65	Tinsley asked him to walk her dog Coco, Matt grabbed the
76	opportunity. Five dollars for a ten-minute walk was a terrific deal.
88	When he asked me to accompany him, I thought, "Why
98	not? I have nothing better to do anyway."
106	One dog eventually led to two, because Matt discovered
115	that walking a second pooch was like getting paid double for an
127	identical amount of work. Then we were asked to walk a third
139	and a fourth dog.
143	While strolling with the dogs, we thought, "Why not take
153	on a paper route as well?"
159	"It would be like free money," Matt declared. "It won't take
170	us any more time because we have to go around the neighborhood
182	every day anyway."
185	That's right. We delivered newspapers while we walked the
194	four dogs. Never mind that our ten-minute walk now required an
206	investment of more than an hour. The laziest kid in the universe
218	had become the hardest-working one of all. **226**

Number of words read: _____   **Number of errors made:** _____

© Macmillan/McGraw-Hill

Making a Home in a New Place

Every year, millions of people move to the United States from other countries. To move from one country to another is called *immigration*. Immigrants come from all over the world, and they have many different reasons for packing up their belongings and seeking a home in a new country. They may be looking for better jobs, or they may be fleeing from a land where their freedom was denied. Natural disasters may have forced them to leave. Maybe they are looking for the chance to have a better education. Whatever their reasons, they leave behind friends, a way of life, and many memories.

After an immigrant family moves to the United States, they may decide not to stay in the same city they first arrived at. Many immigrants first try to establish themselves near other family members who had immigrated earlier. Sooner or later, the new immigrants may discover that they would have better opportunities elsewhere. They might prefer living in another town, or even another state.

At the beginning of the last century, for instance, many immigrants came from Europe on vessels that landed in New York City. Quite a few of them remained there. But millions of them headed elsewhere, traveling by train, boat, or car.

Today, a family may travel conveniently by plane. However, they still face the same old-fashioned challenge of making a home in a strange place. A family may move a number of times before they eventually find an appropriate place to live.

1. Why do people immigrate?
2. What are some of the decisions new immigrants need to make?

Oral Fluency Record Sheet

Name _____ Date _____

Oral Reading Accuracy: _____%   Circle: Fall   Winter   Spring

Oral Reading Fluency Score: _____ words correct per minute

Prosody Rubric: (Circle Score) 1 2 3 4

Comprehension Question Responses

#1 _____

#2 _____

Making a Home in a New Place

	Every year, millions of people move to the United States from
11	other countries. To move from one country to another is called
22	*immigration*. Immigrants come from all over the world, and they have
33	many different reasons for packing up their belongings and seeking
43	a home in a new country. They may be looking for better jobs, or they
58	may be fleeing from a land where their freedom was denied. Natural
70	disasters may have forced them to leave. Maybe they are looking for the
83	chance to have a better education. Whatever their reasons, they leave
94	behind friends, a way of life, and many memories.
103	After an immigrant family moves to the United States, they
113	may decide not to stay in the same city they first arrived at.
126	Many immigrants first try to establish themselves near other family
136	members who had immigrated earlier. Sooner or later, the new
146	immigrants may discover that they would have better opportunities
155	elsewhere. They might prefer living in another town, or even
165	another state.
167	At the beginning of the last century, for instance, many
177	immigrants came from Europe on vessels that landed in New York
188	City. Quite a few of them remained there. But millions of them
200	headed elsewhere, traveling by train, boat, or car.
208	Today, a family may travel conveniently by plane. However,
217	they still face the same old-fashioned challenge of making a home in
230	a strange place. A family may move a number of times before they
243	eventually find an appropriate place to live. **250**

Number of words read: _____   **Number of errors made:** _____

The Last Frontier

Many people claim that space is the last frontier. By this they mean that every country on Earth has already been discovered and explored. To be true explorers, they say, we must journey to distant planets.

While it may be true that space is an open frontier, plenty of frontier still exists here on our planet. This is because the deepest spots of our planet, deep areas beneath the oceans, are still unexplored. The average depth of the world's oceans is 12,200 feet, but parts of the ocean plunge much deeper. The deepest known spot is in the western Pacific and is 36,198 feet below sea level.

Divers can go only so far with the deep sea breathing equipment we have today. To really reach the ocean's depths, people need to travel in special vehicles especially built for underwater exploration. Only a handful of people have done that.

We know that plant life is rare deep below the ocean's surface. That's because sunlight is necessary for plant survival and solar rays can penetrate only about 660 feet below the surface of the water. Deeper than that, the waters are completely dark and plants are unable to survive. Many sea creatures depend on plants for food. What can we assume then about animal activity in the deep water?

We know that some animals have adapted to life in the dark by becoming luminous, giving off a glow. Other creatures have become scavengers, feeding on whatever drops to the ocean floor. But these are just scattered pieces of information. Perhaps one day you will become an underwater explorer and uncover even more secrets of the deep sea.

1. In the author's opinion, what really is the last frontier?
2. Why don't we know more about life at the bottom of the ocean?

© Macmillan/McGraw-Hill

Oral Reading Fluency Grades 1–6

Oral Fluency Record Sheet

Name _____ Date _____

Oral Reading Accuracy: _____%   Circle: Fall   Winter   Spring

Oral Reading Fluency Score: _____ words correct per minute

Prosody Rubric: (Circle Score) 1 2 3 4

Comprehension Question Responses

#1 _____

#2 _____

The Last Frontier

	Many people claim that space is the last frontier. By this
11	they mean that every country on Earth has already been discovered
22	and explored. To be true explorers, they say, we must journey to
34	distant planets.
36	While it may be true that space is an open frontier, plenty
48	of frontier still exists here on our planet. This is because the
60	deepest spots of our planet, deep areas beneath the oceans, are still
72	unexplored. The average depth of the world's oceans is 12,200 feet,
83	but parts of the ocean plunge much deeper. The deepest known
94	spot is in the western Pacific and is 36,198 feet below sea level.
107	Divers can go only so far with the deep sea breathing
118	equipment we have today. To really reach the ocean's depths,
128	people need to travel in special vehicles especially built for
138	underwater exploration. Only a handful of people have done that.
148	We know that plant life is rare deep below the ocean's
159	surface. That's because sunlight is necessary for plant survival and
169	solar rays can penetrate only about 660 feet below the surface of
181	the water. Deeper than that, the waters are completely dark and
192	plants are unable to survive. Many sea creatures depend on plants
203	for food. What can we assume then about animal activity in the
215	deep water?
217	We know that some animals have adapted to life in the dark
229	by becoming luminous, giving off a glow. Other creatures have
239	become scavengers, feeding on whatever drops to the ocean floor.
249	But these are just scattered pieces of information. Perhaps one day
260	you will become an underwater explorer and uncover even more
270	secrets of the deep sea. **275**

Number of words read: _____   **Number of errors made:** _____

© Macmillan/McGraw-Hill

Odysseus and the Sirens

Odysseus was a distinguished Greek hero celebrated in many legends. One of these legends tells about an adventure Odysseus had while sailing home from Troy.

Odysseus knew that he and his crew would have to pass perilously close to the island of the Sirens. The Sirens were a dangerous group of singers whose voices were extremely beautiful. Every time a ship got close to the island, the Sirens would deliberately stand on a hilltop, waving and singing rhythmically. The ship's crew would forget about steering and head directly for the beautiful melody. Before long, their boat would crash and break against the rocky shore.

Odysseus was a man with common sense. He did not want his boat to be destroyed by the Sirens. He came up with a good plan. He instructed his crew to plug their ears with wax while the ship was steering past the island. Then the crew would not be able to hear the song, and the boat would be safe.

But Odysseus yearned to hear the Sirens' song. So he thought of another scheme. He had the crew strap him tightly to the mast. Then, as the crew rowed near the island, Odysseus listened to the most beautiful music imaginable. He struggled in vain to get free, to throw himself into the water and swim toward the Sirens. Finally, the boat passed the island. The sailors took the wax out of their ears and loosened the knots tying Odysseus. He was exhausted, but safe.

1. What danger did Odysseus face near the island of the Sirens?
2. Why did the crew tie Odysseus to the mast?

Diagnostic Assessment

Oral Fluency Record Sheet

Name _____ Date _____

Oral Reading Accuracy: _____% Circle: Fall Winter Spring
Oral Reading Fluency Score: _____ words correct per minute
Prosody Rubric: (Circle Score) 1 2 3 4
Comprehension Question Responses
#1 _____
#2 _____

Odysseus and the Sirens

	Odysseus was a distinguished Greek hero celebrated in
8	many legends. One of these legends tells about an adventure
18	Odysseus had while sailing home from Troy.
25	Odysseus knew that he and his crew would have to pass
36	perilously close to the island of the Sirens. The Sirens were a
48	dangerous group of singers whose voices were extremely beautiful.
57	Every time a ship got close to the island, the Sirens would
69	deliberately stand on a hilltop, waving and singing rhythmically.
78	The ship's crew would forget about steering and head directly for
89	the beautiful melody. Before long, their boat would crash and
99	break against the rocky shore.
104	Odysseus was a man with common sense. He did not want
115	his boat to be destroyed by the Sirens. He came up with a good
129	plan. He instructed his crew to plug their ears with wax while the
142	ship was steering past the island. Then the crew would not be able
155	to hear the song, and the boat would be safe.
165	But Odysseus yearned to hear the Sirens' song. So he
175	thought of another scheme. He had the crew strap him tightly to
187	the mast. Then, as the crew rowed near the island, Odysseus
198	listened to the most beautiful music imaginable. He struggled in
208	vain to get free, to throw himself into the water and swim toward
221	the Sirens. Finally, the boat passed the island. The sailors took the
233	wax out of their ears and loosened the knots tying Odysseus. He
245	was exhausted, but safe. **249**

Number of words read: _____   Number of errors made: _____

© Macmillan/McGraw-Hill

Egyptian Writing

Egyptian picture writing, or hieroglyphics, began almost 5,000 years ago. At first, the Egyptians just drew pictures to stand for objects. For example, the sun was a circle with a dot in it. A house was a small rectangle. Over time, it became too difficult to come up with a new picture for each word. So the Egyptians began to combine words to make sounds. For example, the Egyptian word for "go out" sounds like the words for "house" and "sun." Writers just combined these two pictures when they needed to write the word that means "go out."

Over the centuries, the ability to understand Egyptian writing was lost. Experts puzzled over Egyptian texts without any idea of what they meant. Then, in 1799, an officer in the French army found the Rosetta Stone in Egypt. The strange black stone had three sections of writing carved into it. The first section was a story in Greek. The other two sections were translations of the same story into Egyptian picture writing. Using these translations, experts quickly decoded the Rosetta Stone. Using what they deciphered, they soon solved the puzzle of Egyptian hieroglyphics.

Picture writing was used for thousands of years. But by 1000 B.C., the Phoenicians, a people who also lived in the Middle East, created a less clumsy writing system. Instead of combining pictures to make sounds, they developed an alphabet. Each letter in the alphabet stood for a sound. To form words, several sounds were blended together. The alphabet that we use today comes from the original Phoenician alphabet.

1. How is ancient Egyptian writing different from the way we write?

2. What is the importance of the Rosetta Stone?

© Macmillan/McGraw-Hill

Diagnostic Assessment

Oral Fluency Record Sheet

Name _____ Date _____

Oral Reading Accuracy: _____%   Circle: Fall   Winter   Spring

Oral Reading Fluency Score: _____ words correct per minute

Prosody Rubric: (Circle Score) 1 2 3 4

Comprehension Question Responses

#1 _____

#2 _____

Egyptian Writing

	Egyptian picture writing, or hieroglyphics, began almost
7	5,000 years ago. At first, the Egyptians just drew pictures to stand
19	for objects. For example, the sun was a circle with a dot in it. A
34	house was a small rectangle. Over time, it became too difficult to
46	come up with a new picture for each word. So the Egyptians began
59	to combine words to make sounds. For example, the Egyptian
69	word for "go out" sounds like the words for "house" and "sun."
81	Writers just combined these two pictures when they needed to write
92	the word that means "go out."
98	Over the centuries, the ability to understand Egyptian
106	writing was lost. Experts puzzled over Egyptian texts without any
116	idea of what they meant. Then, in 1799, an officer in the French
129	army found the Rosetta Stone in Egypt. The strange black stone
140	had three sections of writing carved into it. The first section was a
153	story in Greek. The other two sections were translations of the
164	same story into Egyptian picture writing. Using these translations,
173	experts quickly decoded the Rosetta Stone. Using what they
182	deciphered, they soon solved the puzzle of Egyptian hieroglyphics.
191	Picture writing was used for thousands of years. But by
201	1000 B.C., the Phoenicians, a people who also lived in the Middle
213	East, created a less clumsy writing system. Instead of combining
223	pictures to make sounds, they developed an alphabet. Each letter in
234	the alphabet stood for a sound. To form words, several sounds
245	were blended together. The alphabet that we use today comes from
256	the original Phoenician alphabet. **260**

Number of words read: _____   Number of errors made: _____

2005 National Fluency Norms

Jan Hasbrouck and Gerald Tindal completed an extensive study of oral reading fluency in 2004. The results of their study are published in a technical report entitled, "Oral Reading Fluency: 90 Years of Measurement," which is available on the University of Oregon's Web site, **brt.uoregon.edu/tech_reports.htm**.

This table shows the oral reading fluency rates of students in Grades 1 through 6 as determined by Hasbrouck and Tindal's data.

You can use the information in this table to draw conclusions and make decisions about the oral reading fluency of your students. **Students scoring below the 50th percentile using the average score of two unpracticed readings from grade-level materials need a fluency-building program.** In addition, teachers can use the table to set the long-term fluency goals for their struggling readers.

Average weekly improvement is the average words per week growth you can expect from a student. It was calculated by subtracting the fall score from the spring score and dividing the difference by 32, the typical number of weeks between the fall and spring assessments. For Grade 1, since there is no fall assessment, the average weekly improvement was calculated by subtracting the winter score from the spring score and dividing the difference by 16, the typical number of weeks between the winter and spring assessments.

Grade	Percentile	Fall WCPM*	Winter WCPM*	Spring WCPM*	Avg. Weekly Improvement**
1	90		81	111	1.9
	75		47	82	2.2
	50		23	53	1.9
	25		12	28	1.0
	10		6	15	0.6
2	90	106	125	142	1.1
	75	79	100	117	1.2
	50	51	72	89	1.2
	25	25	42	61	1.1
	10	11	18	31	0.6

*WCPM = Words Correct Per Minute

Oral Reading Fluency Grades 1–6

Grade	Percentile	Fall WCPM*	Winter WCPM*	Spring WCPM*	Avg. Weekly Improvement**
3	90	128	146	162	1.1
	75	99	120	137	1.2
	50	71	92	107	1.1
	25	44	62	78	1.1
	10	21	36	48	0.8
4	90	145	166	180	1.1
	75	119	139	152	1.0
	50	94	112	123	0.9
	25	68	87	98	0.9
	10	45	61	72	0.8
5	90	166	182	194	0.9
	75	139	156	168	0.9
	50	110	127	139	0.9
	25	85	99	109	0.8
	10	61	74	83	0.7
6	90	177	195	204	0.8
	75	153	167	177	0.8
	50	127	140	150	0.7
	25	98	111	122	0.8
	10	68	82	93	0.8
7	90	180	192	202	0.7
	75	156	165	177	0.7
	50	128	136	150	0.7
	25	102	109	123	0.7
	10	79	88	98	0.6
8	90	185	199	199	0.4
	75	161	173	177	0.5
	50	133	146	151	0.6
	25	106	115	124	0.6
	10	77	84	97	0.6

**Average words per week growth

K–6 Diagnostic Assessment

Informal Reading
Inventory

Informal Reading Inventory Grades 1–6

IRI Overview

The **Informal Reading Inventory (IRI)** is an individually-administered diagnostic that assesses a student's reading comprehension and reading accuracy. The IRI measures three reading levels: independent, instructional and frustrational. The independent reading level is when a student reads without help from the teacher. To be independent, the student should accurately decode at least 95% of the words and comprehend 90% of the material. The instructional reading level is reached when a student accurately decodes at least 90% of the words and comprehends at least 60% of the material. To obtain a frustrational level, the student decodes 89% or less of the words and can comprehend only 50% of the material.

At each grade level, there are two fiction and two non-fiction reading passages. These passages alternate between oral reading and silent reading as an IRI tests for both oral and silent reading comprehension. To assess the student's comprehension, there are three literal (L) questions, one vocabulary (V) question, and one interpretive (I) question per passage. On the teacher recording sheet, there is a table for each oral reading passage to help identify the student's reading level. This level is based on a combined score of comprehension points and word recognition errors. For each silent reading passage, the total number of comprehension points is used to determine a reading level.

Informal Reading Inventory

The IRI consists of reading passages, teacher recording sheets, and graded word lists for grades 1–6. The reading passages appear on a reproducible student page. Each passage is ten sentences long and consists of Dolch words in Grades 1–3 and Harris-Jacobsen words in 4–6. The reading difficulty of the passages is near the midpoint of each grade level. There is a teacher recording sheet following each student passage that includes the passage, five questions, and a table to determine the appropriate reading level.

How to Use the IRI

Determine reading levels for both oral and silent reading comprehension. Before a student reads a passage, administer the graded word lists to determine the appropriate grade level. These lists span grades 1–6 and consist of Dolch words, story words, and words that contain appropriate sound-spelling sequences for that level. Teachers should start administering the lists with grade 1 to obtain a general estimate of the student's independent, instructional, and frustrational reading levels.

The correct instructional level is when the student makes one error. Students who make two errors should go back to the previous list and start reading at that level.

Informal Reading Inventory Grades 1–6

Use this grade level to start administering the oral and silent reading passages, and as a quick assessment of basic sight word knowledge, and phonics and structural analysis skills.

Administering the IRI

The IRI is organized by grade level. In order to administer the IRI efficiently, you should be familiar with directions, passages, and questions. To administer the IRI, follow these procedures:

1. Make a copy of all of the graded word lists.

2. Place the grade one word list in front of the student and say, *"Here are some words I would like you to read aloud. Try to read them all, even if you are not sure what some of the words are. Let's begin by reading the words on this list."*

3. If the student is able to easily read these words, this early success may build the student's confidence. If you feel certain that a third-grade student can read above a third-grade level, then begin with a higher list. On the other hand, if a first-grade student misses two words on the first-grade word list, then stop. You should then read the passage aloud and have the student answer the comprehension questions. This activity turns into a listening comprehension inventory. Use the scoring table for the silent reading comprehension passage to determine a reading level for listening comprehension.

4. Record words pronounced correctly with a (✓) mark on the sheet that shows each graded word list. Write incorrect responses on the line next to the word.

5. Have the student continue reading higher-level lists until one error is made.

6. After the student misses two words, stop the testing, collect the test sheets, and complete the results in the graded word list section on the sheet.

7. Follow these directions to score the graded word list.
   - The highest level at which the student misses zero words is the student's independent reading level.
   - The highest level at which the student misses one word is the student's instructional reading level.
   - The highest level at which the student misses two words is the frustrational reading level.
   - If the student scores independent, instructional, or frustrational at more than one level, assign the score to the highest level.

8. Select the first passage for the student to read orally. Have the student start reading on the instructional level determined by the graded word lists.

Informal Reading Inventory Grades 1–6

9. Begin by saying, *"I have some passages for you to read. Read the first one aloud. If you find a hard word, try to read it as best you can and continue reading. It is important to remember what you read so you can answer questions at the end."*

10. While the student reads out loud, code the errors or miscues on the scoring sheet. Do not provide any prompting if a student hesitates over a word. If a student hesitates longer than five seconds, simply tell the word to the student.

11. When the student has completed the passage or story, take it away. The student cannot refer to it while answering the questions.

12. Ask the student the comprehension questions as shown on the teacher recording sheet for the passage. Mark correct answers with a point value on the line provided. The point value is in parentheses at the end of each question. A perfect score is 10 points. Interpretive questions are given four points. Vocabulary questions are given three points. Literal questions are given one point. The total number of points that a student earns is the comprehension score. (Instructions for scoring word accuracy and comprehension questions will be provided on page 169.)

At this point, you will have the student shift from oral to silent reading.

13. After scoring the first oral passage, say, *"Read this passage to yourself and try to remember what you read so that you can answer questions at the end."*

14. Give the student the "B" passage next. If the student began with the 1A oral passage, then continue with 1B silent passage.

15. When the student has finished reading the passage, ask the questions based on the passage. Mark the point values that the student earned on the lines provided, and total the number of points earned at the bottom of the questions.

16. After giving the first oral and silent reading passages, determine whether the student has been able to read them at an independent level. If both the oral and silent passages were at the student's independent reading level, continue with the next higher oral reading passage. Then follow with the corresponding silent passage until the frustration level is reached. In many cases, a student will reach frustration level on either oral or silent reading but not both. In these instances, continue with either the oral or silent reading passages until the student reaches frustration level on both.

17. After giving the first oral and silent reading passages, determine if the student is reading at the independent level on either or both passages. If not, give an easier oral and silent passage until both oral and silent frustration levels are reached. The goal is that a student should have an independent, instructional and frustrational reading level for both oral and silent reading.

Diagnostic Assessment

Informal Reading Inventory Grades 1–6

	Code for Marking Word Recognition Errors
Each word recognition error is counted as one error. Never count more than one error on any one word.	
Examples	**Marking Word Recognition Errors**
✓ ✓ ✓ The baby cried	1. Put a check mark over words read correctly.
✓ ✓ My friend (went)	2. Circle omissions.
✓ <u>eats</u> ✓ ✓ He ate the pie	3. Draw a line above words that are read with substitutions. Write the substitution above the line.
✓ T ✓ Why are you	4. Place a <u>T</u> above a word that you need to tell student.
✓ ✓ eating R dinner	5. Place an <u>R</u> next to a word the student repeats.
✓ ✓ ✓ See/S a kind person. She	6. Place the student's initial response and an <u>S</u> above a word that is self corrected. Note: Do not score as an error.
✓ ✓ a (red) apple	7. Use parentheses ( ) to enclose a word that is inserted.

Informal Reading Inventory Grades 1–6

Example of a Passage with Coded Word Recognition Errors

bought
✓ ✓ ✓ ✓ ✓ ✓ ✓ ✓ ✓ ✓ ✓ ✓
Pam went to the store to buy a cake for the surprise party.

✓ ✓ ✓ ✓ ✓ ✓   T
The cake was for her mom's birthday.

✓ ✓ ✓ **T** ✓ ✓ ✓ like/S ch/S
Pam got a chocolate cake. Her R mom (really) loves chocolate.

Here is what the teacher heard as the student read the passage. The words in italics are the actual words that the student read.

"Pam went to the store to bought a cake for the surprise party. The cake was for her mom's birthday. Pam got a (after five seconds the teacher produced "chocolate") cake. Her ... Her mom really likes loves ch ... ch ... chocolate."

The student made four mistakes that are to be scored as errors:

(1) *bought* substituted for *buy*

(2) *birthday* pronounced by the teacher

(3) *chocolate* pronounced by the teacher

(4) *really* inserted

The self correction for *ch* is not counted as an error.

The self correction for *likes* is not counted as an error.

The repetition for *her* is not counted as an error.

This passage is at the frustration level for this student.

Procedure for Scoring Oral Reading Passages

1. Count the total number of scorable errors as outlined in numbers 1–4 and 7 in the **Code for Marking Word Recognition Errors**. Write the total number of errors in the space indicated on the teacher recording sheet. Insertions, substitutions, words told to the student by the teacher, and omissions, are counted as errors at each occurrence. Words that are self-corrected and repeated are not counted as errors.

2. If a student mispronounces a proper name, count it as one error for the entire passage, even if the student mispronounces the same name again.

Informal Reading Inventory Grades 1–6

3. On the teacher recording sheet, a table follows the set of questions for each oral reading passage. Across the table is a series of numbers to designate the number of word recognition errors. In the column on the left hand side is a series of numbers that show the number of points earned. Locate the number of word recognition errors made by the student in that passage and circle the appropriate number. Then locate the number of points earned and draw a circle around that number. Find the point where the two circled numbers intersect. In that space, you will note the following symbols: the (✓) means the student is reading on an independent level; the (∗) means the student is reading on an instructional level; and the (–) means the student is reading at a frustrational level.

Scoring Table for Oral Reading				
Total Points Earned	# of Word Recognition Errors			**Reading Level**
	0–4	**5–7**	**8+**	
7–10 pts	✓	∗	–	Independent ☐
4–6 pts	∗	∗	–	Instructional ☐
0–3 pts	–	–	–	Frustrational ☑

In the above table, for example, the student has made eight word recognition errors and earned two comprehension points. The student answered two literal questions correctly. These two figures intersect in an area marked with a hyphen (–). This means the student is reading on a frustrational level; the box to the right of the frustrational level is checked.

Procedure for Scoring Silent Reading Passages

1. Add up the number of points earned from the five comprehension questions.

2. There is a table below the questions that follow each silent reading passage on the teacher recording sheet. Look at the table to see which level the student is reading at, based on the number of points earned. In the following example, the student earned three points. This would place the student in the range indicated by 0–3 in the table. This corresponds to the frustrational level; the box to the right of the frustrational level is checked.

Scoring Table for Silent Reading	
Total Points Earned	**Reading Level**
7–10 pts	Independent ☐
4–6 pts	Instructional ☐
0–3 pts	Frustrational ☑

Individual Graded Word Lists

Grade 1	Grade 2	Grade 3
mother	prize	started
could	noise	lonely
family	understood	thought
there	another	breathe
said	piece	enough
people	trouble	prepare
bake	easier	actually
what	afraid	waist
three	scare	earn
town	always	delighted

Grade 4	Grade 5	Grade 6
adopted	approaching	countryside
communicate	crystals	heroism
bracelet	development	consented
announced	territory	mercilessly
choice	astonished	appalling
requires	coarse	veterinarian
objects	moisture	spectacle
bulge	luxuries	emperor
gravity	irregular	ravenous
resulting	resemble	exceptional

Recording Sheet for Individual Graded Word Lists

_____ Grade 1 _____

mother _____

could _____

family _____

there _____

said _____

people _____

bake _____

what _____

three _____

town _____

_____ Grade 2 _____

prize _____

noise _____

understood _____

another _____

piece _____

trouble _____

easier _____

afraid _____

scare _____

always _____

_____ Grade 3 _____

started _____

lonely _____

thought _____

breathe _____

enough _____

prepare _____

actually _____

waist _____

earn _____

delighted _____

_____ Grade 4 _____

adopted _____

communicate _____

bracelet _____

announced _____

choice _____

requires _____

objects _____

bulge _____

gravity _____

resulting _____

_____ Grade 5 _____

approaching _____

crystals _____

development _____

territory _____

astonished _____

coarse _____

moisture _____

luxuries _____

irregular _____

resemble _____

_____ Grade 6 _____

countryside _____

heroism _____

consented _____

mercilessly _____

appalling _____

veterinarian _____

spectacle _____

emperor _____

ravenous _____

exceptional _____

Grade 1

mother

could

family

there

said

people

bake

what

three

town

Diagnostic Assessment

Grade 2

prize

noise

understood

another

piece

trouble

easier

afraid

scare

always

Grade 3

started

lonely

thought

breathe

enough

prepare

actually

waist

earn

delighted

Diagnostic Assessment

Grade 4

adopted

communicate

bracelet

announced

choice

requires

objects

bulge

gravity

resulting

Grade 5

approaching

crystals

development

territory

astonished

coarse

moisture

luxuries

irregular

resemble

Diagnostic Assessment

Grade 6

countryside

heroism

consented

mercilessly

appalling

veterinarian

spectacle

emperor

ravenous

exceptional

I A Oral

Sam

Ana was so sad.

She was moving out of town.

They could not take her black cat, Sam.

The new house was just too little for pets.

Ana let a good friend take Sam.

Ana liked her new home, but she missed Sam.

One day, Ana went to open the door.

There was Sam!

He had walked for days and days to find Ana.

Ana's mother now said he could stay.

Diagnostic Assessment

Passage I A Oral—Fiction

Sam

Ana *was so* sad. *She was* moving *out of* town. *They could not take her black* cat, Sam. *The new* house *was just too little for* pets. Ana *let a good* friend *take* Sam.

Ana liked *her new* home, *but she* missed Sam. *One* day, Ana *went to open the* door. *There was* Sam! *He had* walked *for* days *and* days *to find* Ana. Ana's mother *now said he could* stay.

(71 words) (44 Dolch Words) Number of Word Recognition Errors _____

Questions

L 1. _____ Where was Ana moving? [Out of town] (1 pt.)

L 2. _____ Who was Sam? [Ana's black cat] (1 pt.)

L 3. _____ Why couldn't Sam go to the new house? [The new house was too little for pets.] (1 pt.)

V 4. _____ What did the story mean when it said that Ana "missed" Sam? [Ana wished he was with her.] (3 pts.)

I 5. _____ What did Sam do that would make you think he loved Ana? [He walked for days and days to find her.] (4 pts.)

Total # of points earned _____

	Scoring Table for Oral Reading			
	# of Word Recognition Errors			
Total Points Earned	**0–4**	**5–7**	**8+**	**Reading Level**
7–10 pts	✓	*	–	Independent ☐
4–6 pts	*	*	–	Instructional ☐
0–3 pts	–	–	–	Frustrational ☐

I B Silent

The Bake Sale

Mrs. Park's class wanted to help people in need.

Mrs. Park said, "We have to make money.

How can we do this?"

"I know what we can do," Ron said.

"We can bake cakes and other foods people like.

Then, we can have a bake sale."

That is just what the class did.

All the children helped make the food.

A lot of hungry people came to eat it.

Soon, the class had money for people in need.

Diagnostic Assessment

Passage 1B Silent—Fiction

The Bake Sale

Mrs. Park's class wanted to help people in need. Mrs. Park said, "We have to make money. How can we do this?"

"I know what we can do," Ron said. "We can bake cakes and other foods people like. Then, we can have a bake sale."

That is just what the class did. All the children helped make the food. A lot of hungry people came to eat it. Soon, the class had money for people in need.

(78 Words)

Questions

L 1. _____ Who was it that the class wanted to help? [People in need] (1 pt.)

L 2. _____ What did Ron say the class could bake? [Cakes and other foods people like.] (1 pt.)

L 3. _____ What did all the children help to do? [Make the food] (1 pt.)

V 4. _____ The story says, "A lot of hungry people came to eat it." What does *hungry* mean? [Wanting or needing food] (3 pts.)

I 5. _____ Who gave the class the money for the people in need? [The people who paid for food at the bake sale] (4 pts.)

Total # of points earned _____

Scoring Table for Silent Reading	
Total Points Earned	**Reading Level**
7–10 pts	Independent ☐
4–6 pts	Instructional ☐
0–3 pts	Frustrational ☐

I C Oral

School for Clowns

Did you know that there is a clown school?

Clowns go to school to learn to be funny.

They learn how to move in funny ways.

They find out how to run, fall, and jump.

They must make every move look easy.

In school, clowns plan how they will look.

They put on funny pants and tops.

They get into big shoes.

Clowns also put on funny face paint.

They do all this just to make people smile.

Passage I C Oral—Nonfiction

School for Clowns

Did you know that there is a clown school? Clowns *go to* school *to learn to be* funny. They *learn how to* move *in funny* ways. *They find out how to run, fall, and jump. They must make every* move *look* easy. *In* school, clowns plan *how they will look. They put on funny* pants *and* tops. *They get into big* shoes. Clowns also *put on funny* face paint. *They do all this just to make* people smile.

(78 words) (56 Dolch words) Number of Word Recognition Errors _____

Questions

L 1. _____ Why do clowns go to school? [To find out how to be funny] (1 pt.)

L 2. _____ To move in funny ways, clowns find out how to run, jump, and what? [How to fall] (1 pt.)

V 3. _____ The passage says, "They must make every move look easy." What does *easy* mean? [Not hard] (3 pts.)

L 4. _____ Other than funny pants and tops, what do clowns get into? [Big shoes] (1 pt.)

I 5. _____ What is the job of a clown? [To make people smile] (4 pts.)

Total # of points earned _____

	# of Word Recognition Errors			
Scoring Table for Oral Reading				
Total Points Earned	**0–5**	**6–9**	**10+**	**Reading Level**
7–10 pts	✓	*	–	Independent ☐
4–6 pts	*	*	–	Instructional ☐
0–3 pts	–	–	–	Frustrational ☐

I D Silent

Houses

Our houses are places where we feel safe.

It is the place we like to be with our family.

We can stay in when the weather is bad.

We feel good inside our houses.

You can see that all houses are not the same.

There are wood houses and stone houses.

There are even snow houses!

Some houses are big and some are little.

Some have just one floor.

Others are two and even three floors high.

What is the house that you live in like?

Passage 1D Silent—Nonfiction

Houses

Our houses are places where we feel safe. It is the place we like to be with our family. We can stay in when the weather is bad. We feel good inside our houses.

You can see that all houses are not the same. There are wood houses and stone houses. There are even snow houses! Some houses are big and some are little. Some have just one floor. Others are two and even three floors high. What is the house that you live in like?

(86 words)

Questions

L 1. _____ Where do we feel safe? [In our houses] (1 pt.)

L 2. _____ Who do we like to be with in our houses? [Family] (1 pt.)

L 3. _____ How do we feel inside our houses when the weather is bad outside? [Good] (1 pt.)

I 4. _____ Which kind of house would you see in just cold places? [Snow house] (4 pts.)

V 5. _____ The passage says, "Others are two and even three floors high." What does *high* mean? [From top to bottom] (3 pts.)

Total # of points earned _____

Scoring Table for Silent Reading	
Total Points Earned	**Reading Level**
7–10 pts	Independent ☐
4–6 pts	Instructional ☐
0–3 pts	Frustrational ☐

© Macmillan/McGraw-Hill

2A Oral

The Race

One day, Tom saw some boys having a race after school. Tom said, "I would like to be a fast runner like those boys."

Tom began to run every day before and after school. Each day, he was able to run faster than the day before. Soon he could run as fast as the other boys. Tom did not win his first few races, but he would not give up.

The next year, there was a race for all the boys at school. Many of the boys ran fast, but Tom ran faster. The other boys ran hard to catch up with him, but not one could do it. Tom won the race and took home the first prize.

Diagnostic Assessment

Passage 2A Oral—Fiction

The Race

One day, Tom *saw some* boys having *a* race *after* school. Tom *said*, "*I would like to be a fast* runner *like those* boys."

Tom began *to run every* day *before and after* school. Each day, *he was* able *to run* faster than *the* day *before. Soon he could run as fast as the* other boys. Tom *did not* win *his first* few races, *but he would not give up*.

The next year, *there was a* race *for all the* boys *at* school. *Many of the* boys *ran fast, but* Tom *ran* faster. *The* other boys *ran* hard *to* catch *up with him, but not one could do it*. Tom won *the* race *and* took home *the first* prize.

(119 words) (77 Dolch words) Number of Word Recognition Errors _____

Questions

L 1. _____ What did Tom see that made him want to be a fast runner? [Some boys having a race] (1 pt.)

L 2. _____ What did Tom do every day before and after school? [He ran.] (1 pt.)

I 3. _____ What did Tom do that would make you think he sticks with something even if things don't go his way? [He did not win the first few races, but he would not give up.] (4 pts.)

V 4. _____ The story says, "The other boys ran hard to catch up with him, but not one could do it." What does "catch up" mean? [Get closer to, or come up to] (3 pts.)

L 5. _____ Why did Tom take home the first prize? [Because he won the race] (1 pt.)

Total # of points earned _____

Scoring Table for Oral Reading				
	# of Word Recognition Errors			
Total Points Earned	**0–6**	**7–11**	**12+**	**Reading Level**
7–10 pts	✓	*	–	Independent ☐
4–6 pts	*	*	–	Instructional ☐
0–3 pts	–	–	–	Frustrational ☐

2B Silent

Kim and Brownie

Kim had a hard time training her new dog, Brownie. He would not do anything that she told him to do. She could not even get him to come when she called him. Then, one day, Kim saw that Brownie did not move when a loud noise went off.

It was then that she understood that Brownie couldn't hear. Kim found out how to train Brownie by using hand signals. To get Brownie to come, she raised her arm up over her head with her hand facing down.

If she wanted him to sit, she would move her arm down with her hand facing up. Brownie learned fast and was soon doing everything Kim asked of him.

Kim felt very lucky that Brownie was her dog.

Diagnostic Assessment

Passage 2B Silent—Fiction

Kim and Brownie

Kim had a hard time training her new dog, Brownie. He would not do anything that she told him to do. She could not even get him to come when she called him. Then, one day, Kim saw that Brownie would not move when a loud noise went off.

It was then that she understood that Brownie couldn't hear. Kim found out how to train Brownie by using hand signals. To get Brownie to come, she raised her arm up over her head with her hand facing down.

If she wanted him to sit, she would move her arm down with her hand facing up. Brownie learned fast and was soon doing everything Kim asked of him.

Kim felt very lucky that Brownie was her dog.

(126 words)

Questions

L 1. _____ Who was Brownie? [Kim's new dog] (1 pt.)

L 2. _____ What made Kim understand that Brownie couldn't hear? [He would not move when a loud noise went off.] (1 pt.)

V 3. _____ The story says, "Kim found out how to train Brownie by using hand signals." What does the word *signals* mean? [Signs] (3 pts.)

L 4. _____ What signal did Kim use to get Brownie to sit? [Moved her arm down with her hand facing up] (1 pt.)

I 5. _____ What did Brownie do that would make you think he was smart? [He learned fast and was soon doing everything Kim asked of him.] (4 pts.)

Total # of points earned _____

Scoring Table for Silent Reading	
Total Points Earned	**Reading Level**
7–10 pts	Independent ☐
4–6 pts	Instructional ☐
0–3 pts	Frustrational ☐

2C Oral

Bears

Bears are big animals covered with fur. Their legs are short and fat, but they can run very fast. They can also stand up on their back legs and walk like people do.

Bears are mainly colored black, brown, and white. Black bears, which are around five feet, are not as big as brown or white bears. Black and brown bears climb trees to get away from trouble. Both of these bears eat plants, fruit, and animals.

The white bears are called polar bears, and they live on the ice in very cold places. They are great swimmers, and they swim from one piece of ice to another looking for food. These bears eat just meat, and mostly sea animals.

Passage 2C Oral—Nonfiction

Bears

Bears *are big* animals covered *with* fur. *Their* legs *are* short *and* fat, *but they can run very fast. They can* also stand *up on their* back legs *and walk like* people *do.*

Bears *are* mainly colored *black, brown, and white. Black* bears, *which are around five* feet, *are not as big as brown or white* bears. *Black and brown* bears climb trees *to get away from* trouble. *Both of these* bears *eat* plants, fruit, *and* animals.

The white bears *are* called polar bears, *and they live on the* ice *in very cold* places. *They are* great swimmers, *and they* swim *from one* piece *of* ice *to* another looking *for* food. *These* bears *eat just* meat, and mostly sea animals.

(120 words) (75 Dolch words) Number of Word Recognition Errors _____

Questions

L 1. _____ What are bears covered with? [Fur] (1 pt.)

I 2. _____ What does the passage say that lets you know polar bears are over five feet tall? [Black bears, which are around five feet, are not as big as brown or white bears.] (4 pts.)

V 3. _____ The passage says, "Black and brown bears climb trees to get away from trouble." What does the word *trouble* mean? [A bad situation] (3 pts.)

L 4. _____ Where do polar bears live? [On the ice in very cold places] (1 pt.)

L 5. _____ What do polar bears eat? [Meat, mostly sea animals] (1 pt.)

Total # of points earned _____

	Scoring Table for Oral Reading			
	# of Word Recognition Errors			
Total Points Earned	**0–6**	**7–11**	**12+**	**Reading Level**
7–10 pts	✓	*	–	Independent ☐
4–6 pts	*	*	–	Instructional ☐
0–3 pts	–	–	–	Frustrational ☐

2D Silent

About Fire

When people found out how to make fire, their lives became easier. Fire has been around from the days when people lived in caves. Cave people would use fire to stay warm. They also found that they could see more in the dark with the fires going. And many animals like tigers and lions are afraid of fire, so people used fires at night to scare these animals off.

Soon, people found out how to cook over an open fire. Then they made ovens by stacking rocks up over the fires. In these ovens, they baked bread and other good foods. After people found out how to store food, they did not have to go hunting every day. There was always something to eat.

Diagnostic Assessment

Passage 2D Silent—Nonfiction

About Fire

When people found out how to make fire, their lives became easier. Fire has been around from the days when people lived in caves. Cave people would use fire to stay warm. They also found that they could see more in the dark with the fires going. And many animals like tigers and lions are afraid of fire, so people used fires at night to scare these animals off.

Soon, people found out how to cook over an open fire. Then they made ovens by stacking rocks up over the fires. In these ovens, they baked bread and other good foods. After people found out how to store food, they did not have to go hunting every day. There was always something to eat.

(124 words)

Questions

L 1. ____ What happened to people's lives when they found out how to make fire? [Their lives became easier.] (1 pt.)

L 2. ____ What was one way that cave people used fire? [To stay warm, to see in the dark, or to keep animals away] (1 pt.)

V 3. ____ The passage says, "And many animals like tigers and lions are afraid of fire, so people used fires at night to scare these animals off." What does the word *afraid* mean? [Scared] (3 pts.)

L 4. ____ How did people make ovens? [They stacked rocks up over the fires.] (1 pt.)

I 5. ____ After people found out how to cook and store food, what did they eat when they didn't go hunting? [The stored food] (4 pts.)

Total # of points earned _____

Scoring Table for Silent Reading	
Total Points Earned	**Reading Level**
7–10 pts	Independent ☐
4–6 pts	Instructional ☐
0–3 pts	Frustrational ☐

3A Oral

The Dog Walker

Summer vacation had just started, and Earl was thinking about how to spend his time. Earl liked to read, but he didn't want to spend the whole vacation just reading. He also liked to do things and go places with his friends, but many of them were away for the summer. Then Earl got the idea that it would be wise to try to earn some money.

While playing with his dog, Earl suddenly had a thought. Perhaps people would pay him to walk their dogs. Earl went to the houses of people he knew had dogs, like Mrs. Green. Because she was old and had trouble getting around, she was delighted to hire Earl to walk her big brown dog. In all, Earl was able to find seven people to hire him. By the end of the summer, he was able to buy a new bike.

Diagnostic Assessment

Passage 3A Oral—Fiction

The Dog Walker

Summer vacation *had just* started, *and* Earl *was* thinking *about how to* spend *his* time. Earl liked *to read, but he* didn't *want to* spend *the* whole vacation *just* reading. *He* also liked *to do* things *and go* places *with his* friends, *but many of them were away for the* summer. *Then* Earl *got the* idea *that it would be* wise *to try to* earn *some* money.

While playing *with his* dog, Earl suddenly *had a* thought. Perhaps people *would* pay *him to walk their* dogs. Earl *went to the* houses *of* people *he* knew *had* dogs, *like* Mrs. Green. *Because she was old and had* trouble getting *around, she was* delighted *to* hire Earl *to walk her big brown* dog. *In all*, Earl *was* able *to find seven* people *to* hire *him. By the* end *of the* summer, *he was* able *to buy a new* bike.

(147 words) (92 Dolch Words) Number of Word Recognition Errors _____

Questions

L 1. _____ Why couldn't Earl spend time with his friends? [Because many were away for the summer] (1 pt.)

L 2. _____ What was Earl doing when he thought about walking dogs for money? [Playing with his dog] (1 pt.)

V 3. _____ The story says, "Because she was old and had trouble getting around, she was delighted to hire Earl to walk her big brown dog." What does the word *delighted* mean? [Very happy] (3 pts.)

L 4. _____ How many people hired Earl? [Seven] (1 pt.)

I 5. _____ Where did Earl get the money to pay for his new bike? [From walking the dogs] (4 pts.)

Total # of points earned _____

Scoring Table for Oral Reading				
	# of Word Recognition Errors			
Total Points Earned	**0–8**	**9–14**	**15+**	**Reading Level**
7–10 pts	✓	*	–	Independent ☐
4–6 pts	*	*	–	Instructional ☐
0–3 pts	–	–	–	Frustrational ☐

3B Silent

Lonely Nina

Nina had never felt as lonely as she did at her new school. She had moved to town over a month ago, and she still had not made any friends. As she sat eating her lunch, she listened to Jen and the other girls from her class talk and laugh. Afraid that they wouldn't like her, she thought it best to keep to herself.

All of a sudden, Nina heard Jen start to choke on some food. When she saw that the girl couldn't breathe, Nina rushed over. She put her arms around Jen's waist from the back and pressed in with her fist. The food came out, and Jen began to take in air.

When she could talk, Jen thanked Nina and asked her to join the other girls. "I would have asked you before," Jen said, "but you always seemed to want to be by yourself."

© Macmillan/McGraw-Hill

Passage 3B Silent—Fiction

Lonely Nina

Nina had never felt as lonely as she did at her new school. She had moved to town over a month ago, and she still had not made any friends. As she sat eating her lunch, she listened to Jen and the other girls from her class talk and laugh. Afraid that they wouldn't like her, she thought it best to keep to herself.

All of a sudden, Nina heard Jen start to choke on some food. When she saw that the girl couldn't breathe, Nina rushed over. She put her arms around Jen's waist from the back and pressed in with her fist. The food came out, and Jen began to take in air.

When she could talk, Jen thanked Nina and asked her to join the other girls. "I would have asked you before," Jen said, "but you always seemed to want to be by yourself."

(148 words)

Questions

L 1. ____ How did Nina feel at the beginning of the story? [Lonely] (1 pt.)

L 2. ____ Why did Nina keep to herself? [Because she was afraid the other children wouldn't like her] (1 pt.)

V 3. ____ The story says, "When she saw that the girl couldn't breathe, Nina rushed over." What does the word *breathe* mean? [Take in air] (3 pts.)

L 4. ____ What did Jen do as soon as she could talk? [Jen thanked Nina and asked her to join the other girls.] (1 pt.)

I 5. ____ Why didn't Nina make friends? [Because she kept to herself and did not try to talk to the other children] (4 pts.)

Total # of points earned _____

Scoring Table for Silent Reading	
Total Points Earned	**Reading Level**
7–10 pts	Independent ☐
4–6 pts	Instructional ☐
0–3 pts	Frustrational ☐

3C Oral

A Biography

In 1892 a 13-year-old boy beat 25 men to win his first bike race. The boy was Marshall Taylor, and he would become one of the best racers of all time.

Just four years after winning his first race, Taylor became the first black man in the United States to race for money. By the time he was 20 years old, he was setting many records for speed. Sadly, he was not allowed to enter some races because of the color of his skin.

In the years that followed, Taylor raced all over the world. He won almost every race he entered. Millions of people came to see him, and he made friends everywhere he went. Taylor would stop racing in 1924 at the age of 32. But before he did, he broke every speed record there was to earn the title of the fastest bike racer in the world.

Passage 3C Oral—Nonfiction

A Biography

In 1892 *a* 13-year-old boy beat 25 men *to* win *his first* bike race. *The* boy *was* Marshall Taylor, *and he would become one of the best* racers *of all* time.

Just four years *after* winning *his first* race, Taylor became *the first black* man *in the* United States *to* race *for* money. *By the* time *he was* 20 years old, *he was* setting *many* records *for* speed. Sadly, *he was not* allowed *to* enter *some* races *because of the* color *of his* skin.

In the years *that* followed, Taylor raced *all over the* world. *He* won almost *every* race *he* entered. Millions *of* people *came to see him, and he made* friends everywhere *he went.* Taylor *would stop* racing *in* 1924 *at the* age *of* 32. *But before he did, he* broke *every* speed record *there was to* earn *the* title *of the* fastest bike racer *in the* world.

(150 words) (86 Dolch words) Number of Word Recognition Errors _____

Questions

L 1. _____ How old was Taylor when he won his first bike race? [13] (1 pt.)

L 2. _____ What was Taylor the first black man to do? [Race for money] (1 pt.)

V 3. _____ What is skin? [Outer covering of the human body] (3 pts.)

I 4. _____ What happened that would make you think Taylor was popular?
[Millions of people came to see him, and he made friends everywhere he went.] (4 pts.)

L 5. _____ In what year did Taylor stop racing? [1924] (1 pt.)

Total # of points earned _____

Scoring Table for Oral Reading				
Total Points Earned	**# of Word Recognition Errors**			**Reading Level**
	0–8	**9–15**	**16+**	
7–10 pts	✓	*	–	Independent ☐
4–6 pts	*	*	–	Instructional ☐
0–3 pts	–	–	–	Frustrational ☐

© Macmillan/McGraw-Hill

3D Silent

Sleep

People of all ages need to sleep, but some need more sleep than others do. As people grow older, they need less sleep. Babies sleep about 15 hours a day, while adults need about 8 hours of sleep every night.

Sleep is very important because it will give the body and mind time to rest and prepare for the next day. During the early stages of sleep, the heart does not beat as fast and the brain slows down. If a person dreams while asleep, the heart begins beating faster and the brain goes back into action. At this stage of sleep, your eyes move back and forth very fast under your closed lids.

When people don't get enough sleep, they may be hard to get along with. They also may have trouble thinking and doing things. After five days with no sleep, people will start to see things that are not actually there.

Passage 3D Silent—Nonfiction

Sleep

People of all ages need to sleep, but some need more sleep than others do. As people grow older, they need less sleep. Babies sleep about 15 hours a day, while adults need about 8 hours of sleep every night.

Sleep is very important because it will give the body and mind time to rest and prepare for the next day. During the early stages of sleep, the heart does not beat as fast and the brain slows down. If a person dreams while asleep, the heart begins beating faster and the brain goes back into action. At this stage of sleep, your eyes move back and forth very fast under your closed lids.

When people don't get enough sleep, they may be hard to get along with. They also may have trouble thinking and doing things. After five days with no sleep, people will start to see things that are not actually there.

(154 words)

Questions

I 1. _____ From the passage, you can tell that children sleep somewhere between 8 hours and how many hours? [15] (4 pts.)

L 2. _____ Why is sleep important? [Because it will give the body and mind time to rest and prepare for the next day] (1 pt.)

L 3. _____ What happens to your eyes when you dream? [They move back and forth very fast under your closed lids.] (1 pt.)

L 4. _____ What is one thing that may happen to people when they don't get enough sleep? [They may be hard to get along with, they may have trouble thinking, or they may have trouble doing things.] (1 pt.)

V 5. _____ The reading passage says, "After five days with no sleep, people will start to see things that are not actually there." What does the word *actually* mean? [Really] (3 pts.)

Total # of points earned _____

Scoring Table for Silent Reading	
Total Points Earned	**Reading Level**
7–10 pts	Independent ☐
4–6 pts	Instructional ☐
0–3 pts	Frustrational ☐

4A Oral

A Feel for Music

Having a real feel for music, Cora loved to play the piano for friends and family. The problem was that she made mistakes because she never found enough time to sit down and practice.

One day, Mrs. Ruiz, the music teacher, announced that there was going to be a concert, and she wanted Cora to play a piece of music of her choice. Very excited, Cora decided to play "My Favorite Things."

Mrs. Ruiz called all of the children to her house to play their pieces a few days before the concert. To Cora's horror, Matt had decided to play "My Favorite Things" too. Matt played the piece perfectly, but he did not put any feeling into his music. However, all Cora could think was that he would play without any mistakes, while she would make mistakes and look silly.

The next day, Cora told Mrs. Ruiz that she did not want to be in the concert. The teacher said sadly, "You are a very good player because you feel the music, but this means little unless you believe in your talent and give it the time it requires."

Passage 4A Oral—Fiction

A Feel for Music

Having *a* real feel *for* music, Cora loved *to play the* piano *for* friends *and* family. *The* problem *was that she made* mistakes *because she never* found enough time *to sit down and* practice.

One day, Mrs. Ruiz, *the* music teacher, announced *that there was going to be a* concert, *and she* wanted Cora *to play a* piece *of* music *of her* choice. *Very* excited, Cora decided *to play "My* Favorite Things."

Mrs. Ruiz called *all of the* children *to her* house *to play their* pieces *a few days before the* concert. *To* Cora's horror, Matt *had* decided *to play* "My Favorite Things" *too*. Matt played *the* piece perfectly, *but he did not put any* feeling *into his* music. However, *all* Cora *could* think *was that he would play* without any mistakes, while *she would make* mistakes *and look* silly.

The next day, Cora told Mrs. Ruiz *that she did not want to be in the* concert. *The* teacher *said* sadly, *"You are a very good* player *because you* feel *the* music, *but this* means *little* unless *you* believe *in your* talent *and give it the* time *it* requires."

(189 words) (107 Dolch Words) Number of Word Recognition Errors _____

Questions

L 1. _____ Why did Cora make mistakes when she played? [Because she didn't practice enough] (1 pt.)

L 2. _____ What song did Cora choose to play at the concert? ["My Favorite Things"] (1 pt.)

L 3. _____ Where did the children go a few days before the concert to play their pieces? [To Mrs. Ruiz's house] (1 pt.)

V 4. _____ What does the word *horror* mean in this story? [Shock or disappointment] (3 pts.)

I 5. _____ Why did Cora decide not to be in the concert? [Because she was afraid of looking foolish if Matt played the song better than she did] (4 pts.)

Total # of points earned _____

	Scoring Table for Oral Reading			
	# of Word Recognition Errors			
Total Points Earned	**0–11**	**12–18**	**19+**	**Reading Level**
7–10 pts	✓	*	–	Independent ☐
4–6 pts	*	*	–	Instructional ☐
0–3 pts	–	–	–	Frustrational ☐

4B Silent

The Bracelet

Mrs. Dell was delighted when her children gave her a very special present for her birthday. It was a beautiful gold bracelet with five charms, one charm from each of her five children. The clasp on the bracelet was a bit loose, but she planned to have that fixed just as soon as she could get around to it.

Not willing to take the bracelet off, Mrs. Dell wore it always, whether she was at work or doing the household chores. One night before she went to bed, she noticed that the bracelet was not on her wrist. Frantic, she looked for it everywhere, but she just couldn't find it. Feeling miserable, she told the children that she had lost their special gift.

Fifteen years later, all of Mrs. Dell's children were grown and out of the house, so she decided to sell it. The movers had just removed the last piece of furniture, the big sofa, when Mrs. Dell noticed something shiny on the floor. There was her lost bracelet, just like a special gift all over again.

Passage 4B Silent—Fiction

The Bracelet

Mrs. Dell was delighted when her children gave her a very special present for her birthday. It was a beautiful gold bracelet with five charms, one charm from each of her five children. The clasp on the bracelet was a bit loose, but she planned to have that fixed just as soon as she could get around to it.

Not willing to take the bracelet off, Mrs. Dell wore it always, whether she was at work or doing the household chores. One night before she went to bed, she noticed that the bracelet was not on her wrist. Frantic, she looked for it everywhere, but she just couldn't find it. Feeling miserable, she told the children that she had lost their special gift.

Fifteen years later, all of Mrs. Dell's children were grown and out of the house, so she decided to sell it. The movers had just removed the last piece of furniture, the big sofa, when Mrs. Dell noticed something shiny on the floor. There was her lost bracelet, just like a special gift all over again.

(180 words)

Questions

L 1. _____ For what occasion did Mrs. Dell's children give her the bracelet? [Her birthday] (1 pt.)

L 2. _____ When did Mrs. Dell notice that the bracelet was missing? [One night before she went to bed] (1 pt.)

I 3. _____ What probably caused the bracelet to fall off of Mrs. Dell's wrist? [The loose clasp] (4 pts.)

V 4. _____ What does the word *frantic* mean in this story? [Very excited with worry or fear] (3 pts.)

L 5. _____ Where did Mrs. Dell eventually find her bracelet? [On the floor under where the big sofa had been] (1 pt.)

Total # of points earned _____

Scoring Table for Silent Reading	
Total Points Earned	**Reading Level**
7–10 pts	Independent ☐
4–6 pts	Instructional ☐
0–3 pts	Frustrational ☐

4C Oral

Gravity

The force that draws objects toward one another is called gravity. It is the earth's gravity that keeps the moon moving around it and holds the ocean waters against it.

Tides are the rise and fall of large bodies of water. They are caused by the gravity of the moon and the sun, which serves to pull on the waters of the earth. Even though the moon is much smaller than the sun, it has a stronger pull because it is much closer to the earth than the sun is.

When the moon is directly overhead, its gravity causes the waters of the earth to move toward it. As the water follows the moon, the oceans puff out in its direction, resulting in a high tide. When this happens, water rises and can come up onto the land for a short distance. A second bulge occurs on the opposite side of our planet because the earth is also being pulled toward the moon and away from the water on that side. As the moon moves farther away, the water drawn to it will fall back in a low tide.

Passage 4C Oral—Nonfiction

Gravity

The force *that* draws objects toward *one* another *is* called gravity. *It is the* earth's gravity *that* keeps *the* moon moving *around it and* holds *the* ocean waters against *it.*

Tides *are the* rise *and fall of* large bodies *of* water. *They are* caused *by the* gravity *of the* moon *and the* sun, *which* serves *to pull on the* waters *of the* earth. Even though *the* moon *is much* smaller than *the* sun, *it has a* stronger *pull because it is much* closer *to the* earth than *the* sun *is.*

When the moon *is* directly overhead, *its* gravity causes *the* waters *of the* earth *to* move toward *it. As the* water follows *the* moon, *the* oceans puff *out in its* direction, resulting *in a* high tide. *When this* happens, water rises *and can come up* onto *the* land *for a* short distance. A second bulge occurs *on the* opposite side *of our* planet *because the* earth *is* also being pulled toward *the* moon *and away from the* water *on that* side. *As the* moon moves farther *away, the* water drawn *to it will fall* back *in a* low tide.

(189 words) (102 Dolch words) Number of Word Recognition Errors _____

Questions

L 1. _____ What keeps the moon moving around the earth and holds the ocean waters against the earth? [Gravity] (1 pt.)

L 2. _____ Why does the moon have a greater pull on the earth's water than the sun does? [Because the moon is much closer to earth] (1 pt.)

L 3. _____ What causes a high tide? [Ocean waters puff out toward the moon when it is directly overhead.] (1 pt.)

V 4. _____ What is a *bulge*? [A part that swells out] (3 pts.)

I 5. _____ Why does the moon affect tides more than the sun does? [Because the moon is closer to Earth and has a stronger pull.] (4 pts.)

Total # of points earned _____

Scoring Table for Oral Reading				
	# of Word Recognition Errors			
Total Points Earned	**0–11**	**12–18**	**19+**	**Reading Level**
7–10 pts	✓	*	–	Independent ☐
4–6 pts	*	*	–	Instructional ☐
0–3 pts	–	–	–	Frustrational ☐

4D Silent

A Biography of Sequoya

Born around 1765, Sequoya was a member of the Cherokee tribe. He was always fascinated by the white people's ability to communicate with one another by making marks on paper, which he would call "talking leaves." In 1809, he decided that the Cherokee should have a written language of their own. In spite of constant teasing by friends and family, Sequoya gave 12 years of his life to creating an alphabet for his people.

Sequoya found out that the Cherokee language was made up of a particular group of sounds. His alphabet gave a symbol for each of these sounds, resulting in 85 letters in all.

In 1821, Sequoya showed the leading men of the Cherokee Nation how his new alphabet worked. These wise men at once recognized the great worth of the alphabet and quickly adopted it for their people. In just a matter of months, thousands of Cherokee were able to read and write their own language for the first time. Because of Sequoya's vision, the Cherokee could now keep a written record of their great history to be handed down to generations to come.

Passage 4D Silent—Nonfiction

A Biography of Sequoya

Born around 1765, Sequoya was a member of the Cherokee tribe. He was always fascinated by the white people's ability to communicate with one another by making marks on paper, which he would call "talking leaves." In 1809, he decided that the Cherokee should have a written language of their own. In spite of constant teasing by friends and family, Sequoya gave 12 years of his life to creating an alphabet for his people.

Sequoya found out that the Cherokee language was made up of a particular group of sounds. His alphabet gave a symbol for each of these sounds, resulting in 85 letters in all.

In 1821, Sequoya showed the leading men of the Cherokee Nation how his new alphabet worked. These wise men at once recognized the great worth of the alphabet and quickly adopted it for their people. In just a matter of months, thousands of Cherokee were able to read and write their own language for the first time. Because of Sequoya's vision, the Cherokee could now keep a written record of their great history to be handed down to generations to come.

(187 words)

Questions

L 1. ____ What were "talking leaves"? [What Sequoya called the marks on paper used by white people to communicate with one another] (1 pt.)

L 2. ____ What did Sequoya spend 12 years of his life doing? [Creating an alphabet for his people] (1 pt.)

V 3. ____ What does the word *adopted* mean in this passage? [Accepted] (3pts.)

I 4. ____ How do you know that Sequoya's alphabet was easy to use? [In just a matter of months, thousands of Cherokee were able to read and write their own language for the first time.] (4 pts.)

L 5. ____ What did Sequoya's alphabet allow the Cherokee to do? [Keep a written record of their history to be handed down to generations to come] (1 pt.)

Total # of points earned _____

Scoring Table for Silent Reading	
Total Points Earned	**Reading Level**
7–10 pts	Independent ☐
4–6 pts	Instructional ☐
0–3 pts	Frustrational ☐

© Macmillan/McGraw-Hill

5A Oral

The Wolf and the Dog

A scrawny wolf was almost dead with hunger when he happened to meet a house dog who was passing by. "Cousin," said the dog, "your irregular life will soon be the ruin of you. Why don't you work steadily as I do, and get your food regularly given to you?"

"I would have no objection," said the wolf, "if I could only get a place."

"I will arrange that for you if you come with me to my master and share my work," said the dog.

So the wolf and dog went towards the town together. On the way there, the wolf noticed that the hair on a certain part of the dog's neck was very much worn away, so he asked him how that had come about.

"Oh," said the dog, "that is only the place where the collar is put on at night to keep me chained up. It does irritate the neck a bit, but you'll soon get used to it."

"Goodbye to you," said the wolf, "for it is better to be free and starve than be a fat slave."

© Macmillan/McGraw-Hill

Passage 5A Oral—Fiction

The Wolf and the Dog

A scrawny wolf was almost dead with hunger when he happened to meet a house dog who was passing by. "Cousin," said the dog, "your irregular life will soon be the ruin of you. Why don't you work steadily as I do, and get your food regularly given to you?"

"I would have no objection," said the wolf, "if I could only get a place."

"I will arrange that for you if you come with me to my master and share my work," said the dog.

So the wolf and dog went towards the town together. On the way there the wolf noticed that the hair on a certain part of the dog's neck was very much worn away, so he asked him how that had come about.

"Oh," said the dog, "that is only the place where the collar is put on at night to keep me chained up. It does irritate the neck a bit, but you'll soon get used to it."

"Goodbye to you," said the wolf, "for it is better to be free and starve than be a fat slave."

(184 Words) Number of Word Recognition Errors _____

Questions

L 1. _____ Why was the wolf almost dead? [Lack of food] (1 pt.)

I 2. _____ What did the dog do that would make you think he liked the wolf? [He offered to arrange for the wolf to work for his master.] (4 pts.)

L 3. _____ Why was the hair on the dog's neck worn away? [He had to wear a collar at night.] (1 pt.)

V 4. _____ What does the word *irritate* mean in this story? [Make sore] (3 pts.)

L 5. _____ Why does the wolf say goodbye to the dog? [Because he'd rather starve than be chained up] (1 pt.)

Total # of points earned _____

Scoring Table for Oral Reading				
	# of Word Recognition Errors			
Total Points Earned	**0–10**	**11–18**	**19+**	**Reading Level**
7–10 pts	✓	*	–	Independent ☐
4–6 pts	*	*	–	Instructional ☐
0–3 pts	–	–	–	Frustrational ☐

5B Silent

Tracy's Find

Life in Tracy's household became very challenging after her father lost his job. Now the entire family had to watch what they spent, and simple pleasures like buying new clothes or eating out were luxuries that Tracy rarely enjoyed.

With winter fast approaching and Tracy in desperate need of boots, she and her mother visited the used clothing store. Embarrassed and miserable, Tracy searched through the boots until she spied a pair in her size that weren't too worn. When she picked one up to try it on, she noticed something stuffed inside. She was stunned when she stuck in her hand and pulled out a little over $1000 in cash.

Thrilled, she raced over to her mother and said excitedly, "Mom, I found all this money in these boots! The person who gave the boots away won't miss it, so we can keep it, can't we?"

Tracy's mother didn't respond, but the sad and disappointed expression on her face spoke volumes. Ashamed of herself, Tracy knew what her mother expected of her, and she did not hesitate to do it.

Passage 5B Silent—Fiction

Tracy's Find

Life in Tracy's household became very challenging after her father lost his job. Now the entire family had to watch what they spent, and simple pleasures like buying new clothes or eating out were luxuries that Tracy rarely enjoyed.

With winter fast approaching and Tracy in desperate need of boots, she and her mother visited the used clothing store. Embarrassed and miserable, Tracy searched through the boots until she spied a pair in her size that weren't too worn. When she picked one up to try it on, she noticed something stuffed inside. She was stunned when she stuck in her hand and pulled out a little over $1000 in cash.

Thrilled, she raced over to her mother and said excitedly, "Mom, I found all this money in these boots! The person who gave the boots away won't miss it, so we can keep it, can't we?"

Tracy's mother didn't respond, but the sad and disappointed expression on her face spoke volumes. Ashamed of herself, Tracy knew what her mother expected of her, and she did not hesitate to do it.

(181 words)

Questions

L 1. ____ Why did life in Tracy's household become challenging? [Because her father lost his job] (1 pt.)

L 2. ____ Why was Tracy in the used clothing store? [She needed boots for winter.] (1 pt.)

V 3. ____ What does the word *stunned* mean in this story? [Amazed] (3 pts.)

L 4. ____ What did Tracy want to do with the money she found? [Keep it] (1 pt.)

I 5. ____ What did Tracy's mother expect her to do? [Return the money] (5 pts.)

Total # of points earned _____

Scoring Table for Silent Reading	
Total Points Earned	**Reading Level**
7–10 pts	Independent ☐
4–6 pts	Instructional ☐
0–3 pts	Frustrational ☐

© Macmillan/McGraw-Hill

5C Oral

Clouds

Throughout history, people have found clouds to be both interesting and beautiful. Clouds begin to form when warm, damp air is pushed up by cool, dry air. As the warm air rises, it begins to expand and cool. The cooling air is no longer able to hold all of the moisture in gas form that it was able to hold when it was warm. Eventually, tiny drops of water or ice crystals begin to form on bits of dust, taking the shape of a cloud. After the drops or ice crystals form, they can collide with each other and grow by joining together to such a large size that they fall to the ground as rain or snow.

There are four basic families of clouds, with each forming at a different distance above the earth. High clouds form above 20,000 feet, middle clouds appear between 6,500 feet and 20,000 feet, and low clouds appear below 6,500 feet. Finally, there are clouds that are moving upward while their bases are near the ground. These clouds with vertical development range from 1,600 feet to over 20,000 feet.

Passage 5C Oral—Nonfiction

Clouds

Throughout history, people have found clouds to be both interesting and beautiful. Clouds begin to form when warm, damp air is pushed up by cool, dry air. As the warm air rises, it begins to expand and cool. The cooling air is no longer able to hold all of the moisture in gas form that it was able to hold when it was warm. Eventually, tiny drops of water or ice crystals begin to form on bits of dust, taking the shape of a cloud. After the drops or ice crystals form, they can collide with each other and grow by joining together to such a large size that they fall to the ground as rain or snow.

There are four basic families of clouds, with each forming at a different distance above the earth. High clouds form above 20,000 feet, middle clouds appear between 6,500 feet and 20,000 feet, and low clouds appear below 6,500 feet. Finally, there are clouds that are moving upward while their bases are near the ground. These clouds with vertical development range from 1,600 feet to over 20,000 feet.

(185 words) Number of Word Recognition Errors _____

Questions

L 1. _____ What happens to the warm air as it rises? [It begins to expand and cool.] (1 pt.)

V 3. _____ What does the word *moisture* mean in this reading passage? [Wetness] (3 pts.)

L 2. _____ What makes the shape of a cloud? [Tiny drops of water or ice crystals forming on bits of dust] (1 pt.)

L 4. _____ At what distance above earth do middle clouds appear? [Between 6,500 feet and 20,000 feet] (1 pt.)

I 5. _____ Which family of clouds would produce the tallest clouds? [Clouds with vertical development] (4 pts.)

Total # of points earned _____

Scoring Table for Oral Reading				
	# of Word Recognition Errors			
Total Points Earned	**0–10**	**11–18**	**19+**	**Reading Level**
7–10 pts	✓	*	–	Independent ☐
4–6 pts	*	*	–	Instructional ☐
0–3 pts	–	–	–	Frustrational ☐

© Macmillan/McGraw-Hill

5D Silent

Deserts

Most people think of a desert as a wide, empty stretch of coarse sand and low dunes. Although some parts of large deserts do resemble this description, there are other regions that do not fit this picture.

To be a desert, a territory must have less than ten inches of rain a year. These dry areas are widely scattered over the earth, covering one-fifth of its land surface. The Sahara is the world's largest desert, stretching 3,200 miles across northern Africa and covering an area almost as large as the United States. The Sahara is the driest and hottest of all the world's deserts, creating one of the harshest environments on Earth.

You might be astonished to learn that only one-fifth of the entire area of the Sahara is covered with sand. If you travel through the Sahara, you'll see snow-capped mountains, such as the Tibesti, which are higher than 10,000 feet. There are also lakes such as Lake Chad, which is the size of the state of New Jersey. Also native to the Sahara are canyons, stony plains, and fifty oases, which are desert areas containing water.

Diagnostic Assessment

Passage 5D Silent—Nonfiction

Deserts

Most people think of a desert as a wide, empty stretch of coarse sand and low dunes. Although some parts of large deserts do resemble this description, there are other regions that do not fit this picture.

To be a desert, a territory must have less than ten inches of rain a year. These dry areas are widely scattered over the earth, covering one-fifth of its land surface. The Sahara is the world's largest desert, stretching 3,200 miles across northern Africa and covering an area almost as large as the United States. The Sahara is the driest and hottest of all the world's deserts, creating one of the harshest environments on Earth.

You might be astonished to learn that only one-fifth of the entire area of the Sahara is covered with sand. If you travel through the Sahara, you'll see snow-capped mountains, such as the Tibesti, which are higher than 10,000 feet. There are also lakes such as Lake Chad, which is the size of the state of New Jersey. Also native to the Sahara are canyons, stony plains, and fifty oases, which are desert areas containing water.

(188 words)

Questions

V 1. _____ What does the word *resemble* mean in this reading passage? [Look like] (3 pts.)

L 2. _____ To be a desert, what must a territory have? [Less than ten inches of rain a year] (1 pt.)

L 3. _____ Where is the Sahara located? [Northern Africa] (1 pt.)

I 4. _____ What in the passage would make you think that relatively few people live in the Sahara? [It is the driest and hottest of all the world's deserts, creating one of the harshest environments on Earth.] (4 pts.)

L 5. _____ How much of the entire area of the Sahara is covered with sand? [One-fifth] (1 pt.)

Total # of points earned _____

Scoring Table for Silent Reading	
Total Points Earned	**Reading Level**
7–10 pts	Independent ☐
4–6 pts	Instructional ☐
0–3 pts	Frustrational ☐

© Macmillan/McGraw-Hill

6A Oral

Androcles and the Lion

A slave named Androcles once escaped from his master and fled to the forest. As he wandered about there, he came upon a lion moaning and groaning in acute pain. At first he turned to flee, but then he saw that the lion's paw was all swollen and bleeding due to the presence of a huge thorn. Androcles pulled out the thorn and bound up the paw, after which the lion licked the man's hand in appreciation and the two became fast friends.

Shortly afterwards both Androcles and the lion were captured, and the slave was sentenced to be thrown to the lion after the latter had not been fed for several days. The emperor and all his court came to see the spectacle, and Androcles was led out into the middle of the arena. Soon the ravenous lion was let loose and rushed roaring toward his victim. But as soon as he approached Androcles, he recognized his friend and licked his hand. The emperor, astounded at this, summoned Androcles to him. After hearing the slave's exceptional story, the emperor freed him and released the lion to his native forest.

Diagnostic Assessment

Passage 6A Oral—Fiction

Androcles and the Lion

A slave named Androcles once escaped from his master and fled to the forest. As he wandered about there, he came upon a lion moaning and groaning in acute pain. At first he turned to flee, but then he saw that the lion's paw was all swollen and bleeding due to the presence of a huge thorn. Androcles pulled out the thorn and bound up the paw, after which the lion licked the man's hand in appreciation and the two became fast friends.

Shortly afterwards both Androcles and the lion were captured, and the slave was sentenced to be thrown to the lion after the latter had not been fed for several days. The emperor and all his court came to see the spectacle, and Androcles was led out into the middle of the arena. Soon the ravenous lion was let loose and rushed roaring toward his victim. But as soon as he approached Androcles, he recognized his friend and licked his hand. The emperor, astounded at this, summoned Androcles to him. After hearing the slave's exceptional story, the emperor freed him and released the lion to his native forest.

(190 words) Number of Word Recognition Errors _____

Questions

L 1. _____ Why was Androcles in the forest? [He fled there after escaping from his master.] (1 pt.)

I 2. _____ What in the story supports the idea that Androcles is both brave and considerate? [He tends to the wounded lion despite the danger.] (4 pts.)

L 3. _____ What was Androcles's sentence after he was captured? [He was to be thrown to the lion after it had not been fed for several days.] (1 pt.)

L 4. _____ Why didn't the lion attack Androcles? [Because he recognized the friend who had helped him in the forest] (1 pt.)

V 5. _____ What does the word *exceptional* mean in this story? [Extraordinary] (3 pts.)

Total # of points earned _____

Scoring Table for Oral Reading				
	# of Word Recognition Errors			
Total Points Earned	**0–11**	**12–19**	**20+**	**Reading Level**
7–10 pts	✓	*	–	Independent ☐
4–6 pts	*	*	–	Instructional ☐
0–3 pts	–	–	–	Frustrational ☐

6B Silent

Morgan's Escape

After making her escape, Morgan glanced nervously around as she slowly moved into the deserted street. Hearing someone approaching from behind, she crouched behind some trash cans and peeked out to see the figure of a man. As he called her name, she recognized the familiar voice of Ben, someone she had once foolishly trusted. He had lost her trust by taking her to that awful place where a woman in a white coat had placed her on a cold table. Luckily, she had managed to escape and make a run for her life.

As Ben stepped closer to the spot where Morgan was hiding, she crouched down lower, hoping that he would not detect her. Frozen with fear, she reacted too late when Ben grabbed her.

Indignant and humiliated, Morgan struggled to be free, but Ben held her resolutely and said, "You shouldn't have run out of the veterinarian's office, you silly cat. Now let's go home so we can both get something to eat." At the mention of food, Morgan decided to forgive Ben and go quietly home with him.

Passage 6B Silent—Fiction

Morgan's Escape

After making her escape, Morgan glanced apprehensively around as she cautiously moved into the deserted street. Hearing someone approaching from behind, she crouched behind some trash cans and peeked out to see the figure of a man. As he called her name, she recognized the familiar voice of Ben, someone she had once foolishly trusted. He had betrayed her trust by taking her to that appalling place where a woman in a white coat had placed her on a cold table. Luckily, she had managed to escape and make a run for her life.

As Ben stepped closer to the spot where Morgan was hiding, she crouched down lower, hoping that he would not detect her. Frozen with fear, she reacted too late when Ben grabbed her.

Indignant and humiliated, Morgan struggled to be free, but Ben held her resolutely and said, "You shouldn't have run out of the veterinarian's office, you silly cat. Now let's go home so we can both get something to eat." At the mention of food, Morgan decided to forgive Ben and go quietly home with him.

(182 words)

Questions

L 1. ____ Where did Morgan hide when she heard someone approaching? [Behind some trash cans] (1 pt.)

L 2. ____ Who was looking for Morgan? [Ben] (1 pt.)

V 3. ____ What does the word *appalling* mean in this story? [Awful] (3 pts.)

I 4. ____ Who was the woman in the white coat? [The veterinarian] (4 pts.)

L 5. ____ Why did Morgan decide to go quietly home with Ben? [He mentioned food.] (1 pt.)

Total # of points earned _____

Scoring Table for Silent Reading	
Total Points Earned	**Reading Level**
7–10 pts	Independent ☐
4–6 pts	Instructional ☐
0–3 pts	Frustrational ☐

© Macmillan/McGraw-Hill

6C Oral

Comets

People have long been both awed and alarmed by comets flashing across the sky. To people of the past who didn't understand the movement of heavenly bodies, the ominous sight of a comet was often linked to terrible events such as wars or plagues. The earliest known record of a comet sighting was made in China around 1059 B.C. Since then, these regular visitors have been observed by astronomers like Edmond Halley, who first proved that comets return as they orbit the sun.

Comets, sometimes called "dirty snowballs," are lumps of dust and rock held together by ice. They orbit the sun in an oval path that brings them very close to it and swings them deep into space. As a dark, cold comet approaches the sun, it goes through a spectacular change. Usually, heated ice turns to water first and then evaporates to form a gas. However, when a comet gets close to the sun, the intense heat changes the surface ice directly into gases, which begin to glow. Fountains of dust and gas squirt out for millions of miles, forming a long tail that glows from reflected sunlight.

Diagnostic Assessment

Passage 6C Oral—Nonfiction

Comets

People have long been both awed and alarmed by comets flashing across the sky. To people of the past who didn't understand the movement of heavenly bodies, the ominous sight of a comet was often linked to terrible events such as wars or plagues. The earliest known record of a comet sighting was made in China around 1059 B.C. Since then, these regular visitors have been observed by astronomers like Edmond Halley, who first proved that comets return as they orbit the sun.

Comets, sometimes called "dirty snowballs," are lumps of dust and rock held together by ice. They orbit the sun in an oval path that brings them very close to it and swings them deep into space. As a dark, cold comet approaches the sun, it goes through a spectacular change. Usually, heated ice turns to water and then evaporates. However, when a comet gets close to the sun, the intense heat changes the surface ice directly into gases, which begin to glow. Fountains of dust and gas squirt out for millions of miles, forming a long tail that glows from reflected sunlight.

(190 words) Number of Word Recognition Errors _____

Questions

V 1. _____ What does the word *ominous* mean in this reading passage? [Threatening or alarming] (3 pts.)

L 2. _____ Who first proved that comets return as they orbit the sun? [Edmond Halley] (1 pt.)

L 3. _____ What are comets made of? [Lumps of dust and rock held together by ice] (1 pt.)

L 4. _____ What does the intense heat of the sun do to the comet? [Changes the surface ice directly into gases, which begin to glow] (1 pt.)

I 5. _____ How does the comet change as it moves away from the sun in its orbit? [It grows cold once more and the ice refreezes.] (4 pts.)

Total # of points earned _____

	Scoring Table for Oral Reading			
	# of Word Recognition Errors			
Total Points Earned	**0–11**	**12–19**	**20+**	**Reading Level**
7–10 pts	✓	*	–	Independent ☐
4–6 pts	*	*	–	Instructional ☐
0–3 pts	–	–	–	Frustrational ☐

© Macmillan/McGraw-Hill

6D Silent

Sybil's Ride

Everyone has heard of Paul Revere's ride to warn a sleeping countryside that the British were coming. About two years later, there was another essential ride—this time made by a girl named Sybil Ludington.

The eldest child of Colonel Henry Ludington, Sybil was with her family in New York on the night of April 26, 1777, when a messenger knocked on the door. He related that the British were burning the town of Danbury, Connecticut, only 25 miles away. With his men scattered over a wide area, Colonel Ludington had to alert them and organize his troops to fend off the British raid. Not being able to do both, he consented to let Sybil ride to summon the men.

It was raining hard that night, but Sybil rode her horse over 40 miles on dark, unmarked roads to notify the men to gather at her home. When, soaked and exhausted, she returned home, most of the soldiers were ready to march. The men whom she gathered arrived in time to drive the British back to their ships in Long Island Sound. After the battle, General George Washington congratulated Sybil for her heroism.

Passage 6D Silent—Nonfiction

Sybil's Ride

Everyone has heard of Paul Revere's ride to warn a sleeping countryside that the British were coming. About two years later, there was another essential ride—this time made by a girl named Sybil Ludington.

The eldest child of Colonel Henry Ludington, Sybil was with her family in New York on the night of April 26, 1777, when a messenger knocked on the door. He related that the British were burning the town of Danbury, Connecticut, only 25 miles away. With his men scattered over a wide area, Colonel Ludington had to alert them and organize his troops to fend off the British raid. Not being able to do both, he consented to let Sybil ride to summon the men.

It was raining hard that night, but Sybil rode her horse over 40 miles on dark, unmarked roads to notify the men to gather at her home. When, soaked and exhausted, she returned home, most of the soldiers were ready to march. The men whom she gathered arrived in time to drive the British back to their ships in Long Island Sound. After the battle, General George Washington congratulated Sybil for her heroism.

(193 words)

Questions

V 1. ___ What does the word *essential* mean in this reading passage? [Very important] (3 pts.)

L 2. ___ What did the messenger tell Sybil and her family? [The British were burning the town of Danbury, Connecticut] (1 pt.)

L 3. ___ What did Colonel Ludington consent to let Sybil do? [Ride to summon the men] (1 pt.)

I 4. ___ How do you know that Sybil was a skillful horsewoman? [Because she successfully rode over 40 miles in the rain and dark over unmarked roads] (4 pts.)

L 5. ___ What did the men whom Sybil gathered succeed in doing? [Driving the British back to their ships in Long Island Sound] (1 pt.)

Total # of points earned _____

Scoring Table for Silent Reading	
Total Points Earned	**Reading Level**
7–10 pts	Independent ☐
4–6 pts	Instructional ☐
0–3 pts	Frustrational ☐

© Macmillan/McGraw-Hill

Informal Reading Inventory Record

Graded Word Lists

	Grade Level	Date Administered
Independent		
Instructional		
Frustrational		

Oral Reading Passage

	Grade Level	Date Administered
Independent		
Instructional		
Frustrational		

Silent Reading Passage

	Grade Level	Date Administered
Independent		
Instructional		
Frustrational		

Comments:

Diagnostic Assessment

K–6 Diagnostic Assessment

Spelling

- *Words Their Way* Qualitative Spelling Inventory

Words Their Way Qualitative Spelling Inventory

Skill Assessed
Spelling

Grade Level
• Primary K–3
• Elementary K–6
• Upper Level, 6–8
• English

Group/individual

Approximate Testing Time
10–15 Minutes

▶ **WHAT** The *Words Their Way Qualitative Spelling Inventory* consists of three inventories: one for primary students in grades K–3, one for elementary students in grades 1–6, and one for upper level students in grades 6–8 and above. The inventories are administered in the same way as a standard spelling test. The focus of this inventory, in contrast to the typical spelling test, is to examine the types of errors made by students as well as to take note of correctly spelled words. Through this examination, the student's skills can be classified as falling into a particular developmental stage of spelling. Bear and his co-authors identify the five developmental spelling stages listed below. A Grouping example of spelling at each stage is also shown.

Materials
Pencil or pen
Lined paper
Source: *Words Their Way: Word Study for Phonics, Vocabulary & Spelling Instruction* by Donald Bear, Marcia Invernizzi, Shane Templeton, and Francine Johnston

Spelling Stages	
Stage 1. Preliterate	Marks on the page
Stage 2. Letter Name	bd for *bed*
Stage 3. Within Word Pattern	*traen* for *train*
Stage 4. Syllable Juncture	*confedent* for *confident*
Stage 5. Derivational Constancy	*emphasize* for *emphasize* (spelled correctly)

© Macmillan/McGraw-Hill

Spelling Grades K-6

▶ **HOW** **General Directions for Administering the Inventories**

Students should not study the words in advance of testing. Assure students that they will not be graded on this activity, and that they will be helping you plan for their needs. Following is a possible introduction to the assessment.

> *I am going to ask you to spell some words. Spell them the best you can. Some of the words may be easy to spell; some may be difficult. When you do not know how to spell a word, spell it the best you can.*

Ask students to number their paper (or prepare a numbered paper for kindergarten or early first grade). Call each word aloud and repeat it. Say each word naturally, with-out emphasizing phonemes or syllables. Use it in a sentence, if necessary, to be sure students know the exact word. Sample sentences are provided along with the words. After administering the inventory, use a Feature Guide, Class Composite Form, and, if desired, a Spelling-by-Stage Classroom Organization Chart to complete your assessment.

Scoring the Inventory Using the Feature Guides

1. Make a copy of the appropriate Feature Guide (PSI pp. 5–6, ESI pp. 10–11, USI pp. 16–17) for each student. Draw a line under the last word called if you called fewer than the total number and adjust the possible total points at the bottom of each feature column.

2. Score the words by checking off the features spelled correctly that are listed in the cells to the left of each word. For example, if a student spells *bed* as *bad*, he gets a check in the initial *b* cell and the final *d* cell, but not for the short vowel. Write in the vowel used (*a*, in this case), but do not give any points for it. If a student spells *train* as *trane*, she gets a check in the initial *tr* cell and the final *n* cell, but not for the long vowel pattern. Write in the vowel pattern used (*a-e* in this case), but do not give any points for it. Put a check in the "Correct" column if the word is spelled correctly. Do not count reversed letters as errors but note them in the cells. If unnecessary letters are added, give the speller credit for what is correct (e.g., if *bed* is spelled *bede*, the student still gets credit for representing the short vowel), but do not check "Correct" spelling.

3. Add the number of checks under each feature and across each word, double-checking the total score recorded in the last cell. Modify the ratios in the last row depending on the number of words called aloud.

Spelling Grades K–6

Interpreting the Results of the Spelling Inventory

1. Look down each feature column to determine instructional needs. Students who miss only one (or two, if the features sample 8 to 10 words) can go on to other features. Students who miss two or three need some review work; students who miss more than three need careful instruction on this feature. If a student did not get any points for a feature, earlier features need to be studied first.

2. To determine a stage of development, note where students first make two or more errors under the stages listed in the shaded box at the top of the Feature Guide. Circle this stage.

Using the Class Composite and Spelling by Stage Form

1. Staple each Feature Guide to the student's spelling paper and arrange the papers in rank order from highest total points to lowest total points.

2. List students' names in this rank order in the left column of the appropriate Classroom Composite (PSI pp. 7–8, ESI pp. 12–13, USI pp. 18–19) and transfer each student's feature scores from the bottom row of the individual Feature Guides to the Classroom Composite. If you do not call out the total list, adjust the totals on the bottom row of the Classroom Composite.

3. Highlight cells where students make two or more errors on a particular feature to get a sense of your groups' needs and to form groups for instruction.

4. Many teachers find it easier to form groups using the Spelling-by-Stage Classroom Organization Chart. List each student under the appropriate spelling stage (the stage circled on the Feature Guide) and determine instructional groups.

Diagnostic Assessment

Primary Spelling Inventory (PSI)

The Primary Spelling Inventory (PSI) is used in kindergarten through third grade. The 26 words are ordered by difficulty to sample features of the letter name-alphabetic to within word pattern stages. Call out enough words so that you have at least five or six misspelled words to analyze. For kindergarten or other emergent readers, you may only need to call out the first five words. In late kindergarten and early first grade classrooms, call out at least 15 words so that you sample digraphs and blends; use the entire list for late first, second, and third grades. If any students spell more than 20 words correctly, you may want to use the Elementary Spelling Inventory.

1. fan — I could use a fan on a hot day. *fan*
2. pet — I have a pet cat who likes to play. *pet*
3. dig — He will dig a hole in the sand. *dig*
4. rob — A raccoon will rob a bird's nest for eggs. *rob*
5. hope — I hope you will do well on this test. *hope*
6. wait — You will need to wait for the letter. *wait*
7. gum — I stepped on some bubble gum. *gum*
8. sled — The dog sled was pulled by huskies. *sled*
9. stick — I used a stick to poke in the hole. *stick*
10. shine — He rubbed the coin to make it shine. *shine*
11. dream — I had a funny dream last night. *dream*
12. blade — The blade of the knife was very sharp. *blade*
13. coach — The coach called the team off the field. *coach*
14. fright — She was a fright in her Halloween costume. *fright*
15. chewed — The dog chewed on the bone until it was gone. *chewed*
16. crawl — You will get dirty if you crawl under the bed. *crawl*
17. wishes — In fairy tales wishes often come true. *wishes*
18. thorn — The thorn from the rosebush stuck me. *thorn*
19. shouted — They shouted at the barking dog. *shouted*
20. spoil — The food will spoil if it sits out too long. *spoil*
21. growl — The dog will growl if you bother him. *growl*
22. third — I was the third person in line. *third*
23. camped — We camped down by the river last weekend. *camped*
24. tries — He tries hard every day to finish his work. *tries*
25. clapping — The audience was clapping after the program. *clapping*
26. riding — They are riding their bikes to the park today. *riding*

Spelling Grades K-6

Words Their Way Primary Spelling Inventory Feature Guide

Student's Name _____ Teacher _____ Grade _____ Date _____

Words Spelled Correctly: ____/26 Feature Points: ____/56 Total: ____/82 Spelling Stage: _____

SPELLING STAGES →	EMERGENT LATE		LETTER NAME-ALPHABETIC EARLY / MIDDLE / LATE			WITHIN WORD PATTERN EARLY / MIDDLE		SYLLABLES AND AFFIXES LATE / EARLY		
Features →	Consonants Initial	Final	Short Vowels	Digraphs	Blends	Long Vowel Patterns	Other Vowels	Inflected Endings	Feature Points	Words Spelled Correctly
1. fan	f	n	a							
2. pet	p	t	e							
3. dig	d	g	i							
4. rob	r	b	o							
5. hope	h	p				o-e				
6. wait	w	t				ai				
7. gum	g	m	u							
8. sled			e		sl					
9. stick			i		st					
10. shine				sh		i-e				
11. dream					dr	ea				
12. blade					bl	a-e				
13. coach				-ch		oa				
14. fright					fr	igh				
15. chewed				ch			ew	-ed		
16. crawl					cr		aw			
17. wishes				-sh				-es		
18. thorn				th			or			

(continued)

© Macmillan/McGraw-Hill

Diagnostic Assessment

© Macmillan/McGraw-Hill

Words Their Way Primary Spelling Inventory Feature Guide

Student's Name _____ Teacher _____ Grade _____ Date _____

Words Spelled Correctly: _____ /26   Feature Points: _____ /56   Total: _____ /82   Spelling Stage: _____

SPELLING STAGES →	EMERGENT LATE	LETTER NAME–ALPHABETIC			WITHIN WORD PATTERN				SYLLABLES AND AFFIXES		
	EARLY	MIDDLE	LATE		EARLY	MIDDLE		LATE	EARLY		
Features →	Consonants Initial · Final	Short Vowels	Digraphs	Blends	Long Vowel Patterns	Other Vowels		Inflected Endings	Feature Points	Words Spelled Correctly
19. shouted			sh			ou		-ed		
20. spoil						oi				
21. growl						ow				
22. third			th			ir				
23. camped								-ed		
24. tries				tr				-ies		
25. clapping								-pping		
26. riding								-ding		
Totals	/7	/7	/7	/7	/7	/7		/7	/56	/26

Words Their Way Primary Spelling Inventory Classroom Composite

Teacher _____   School _____   Grade _____   Date _____

SPELLING STAGES →	EMERGENT LATE		LETTER NAME–ALPHABETIC EARLY MIDDLE LATE			WITHIN WORD PATTERN EARLY MIDDLE LATE			SYLLABLES AND AFFIXES EARLY		
	Consonants		Short Vowels	Digraphs	Blends	Long Vowels	Other Vowels	Inflected Endings	Correct Spelling	Total Rank Order
Students' Name	Initial	Final								
Possible Points	7	7	7	7	7	7	7	7	26	82
1.										
2.										
3.										
4.										
5.										
6.										
7.										
8.										
9.										
10.										
11.										
12.										
13.										
14.										
15.										
16.										
17.										
18.										
19.										

(continued)

Spelling Grades K–6

Words Their Way Primary Spelling Inventory Classroom Composite

Teacher _____ School _____ Grade _____ Date _____

SPELLING STAGES → Students' Name	EMERGENT LATE Consonants Initial	Final	LETTER NAME-ALPHABETIC EARLY MIDDLE LATE Short Vowels	Digraphs	Blends	WITHIN WORD PATTERN EARLY MIDDLE LATE Long Vowels	Other Vowels	SYLLABLES AND AFFIXES LATE EARLY Inflected Endings	Correct Spelling	Total Rank Order
Possible Points	7	7	7	7	7	7	7	7	26	82
20.										
21.										
22.										
23.										
24.						*				
25.										
26.										
Highlight for Instruction*										

*Highlight students who miss more than 1 on a particular feature; they will benefit from more instruction in that area.

Elementary Spelling Inventory (ESI)

The Elementary Spelling Inventory (ESI) covers more stages than the PSI. It can be used as early as first grade, particularly if a school system wants to use the same inventory across the elementary grades. The 25 words are ordered by difficulty to sample features of the letter name-alphabetic to derivational relations stages. Call out enough words so that you have at least five or six misspelled words to analyze. If any students spell more than 20 words correctly, use the Upper Level Spelling Inventory.

1. bed — I hopped out of bed this morning. *bed*
2. ship — The ship sailed around the island. *ship*
3. when — When will you come back? *when*
4. lump — He had a lump on his head after he fell. *lump*
5. float — I can float on the water with my new raft. *float*
6. train — I rode the train to the next town. *train*
7. place — I found a new place to put my books. *place*
8. drive — I learned to drive a car. *drive*
9. bright — The light is very bright. *bright*
10. shopping — She went shopping for new shoes. *shopping*
11. spoil — The food will spoil if it is not kept cool. *spoil*
12. serving — The restaurant is serving dinner tonight. *serving*
13. chewed — The dog chewed up my favorite sweater yesterday. *chewed*
14. carries — She carries apples in her basket. *carries*
15. marched — We marched in the parade. *marched*
16. shower — The shower in the bathroom was very hot. *shower*
17. bottle — The bottle broke into pieces on the tile floor. *bottle*
18. favor — He did his brother a favor by taking out the trash. *favor*
19. ripen — The fruit will ripen over the next few days. *ripen*
20. cellar — I went down to the cellar for the can of paint. *cellar*
21. pleasure — It was a pleasure to listen to the choir sing. *pleasure*
22. fortunate — It was fortunate that the driver had snow tires. *fortunate*
23. confident — I am confident that we can win the game. *confident*
24. civilize — They wanted to civilize the forest people. *civilize*
25. opposition — The coach said the opposition would be tough. *opposition*

Words Their Way Elementary Spelling Inventory Feature

Student's Name _____ Teacher _____ Grade _____ Date _____

Words Spelled Correctly: ____ /25 Feature Points: ____ /62 Total: ____ /87 Spelling Stage: ____

SPELLING STAGES →	EMERGENT LATE EARLY		LETTER NAME-ALPHABETIC EARLY MIDDLE LATE			WITHIN WORD PATTERN EARLY MIDDLE LATE			SYLLABLES AND AFFIXES EARLY MIDDLE LATE			DERIVATIONAL RELATIONS EARLY MIDDLE		
Features →	Consonants Initial	Final	Short Vowels	Digraphs	Blends	Long Vowels	Other Vowels	Inflected Endings	Syllable Junctures	Unaccented Final Syllables	Harder Suffixes	Bases or Roots	Feature Points	Words Spelled Correctly
1. bed	b	d	e											
2. ship		p	i	sh										
3. when			e	wh										
4. lump	l		u		mp									
5. float		t			fl	oa								
6. train		n			tr	ai								
7. place					pl	a-e								
8. drive		v			dr	i-e								
9. bright					br	igh								
10. shopping			o	sh				pping						
11. spoil					sp		oi							
12. serving							er	ving						
13. chewed				ch			ew	ed						
14. carries							ar	ies	rr					
15. marched				ch			ar	ed						
16. shower				sh			ow			er				
17. bottle									tt	le				
18. favor									v	or				

(continued)

© Macmillan/McGraw-Hill

Words Their Way Elementary Spelling Inventory Feature

Student's Name _____ Teacher _____ Grade _____ Date _____

Words Spelled Correctly: ____/25 Feature Points: ____/25 Total: ____/87 Spelling Stage: _____

SPELLING STAGES →	EMERGENT LATE EARLY		LETTER NAME-ALPHABETIC MIDDLE LATE			WITHIN WORD PATTERN EARLY MIDDLE LATE			SYLLABLES AND AFFIXES EARLY MIDDLE LATE		DERIVATIONAL RELATIONS EARLY MIDDLE			
Features →	Consonants Initial	Final	Short Vowels	Digraphs	Blends	Long Vowels	Other Vowels	Inflected Endings	Syllable Junctures	Unaccented Final Syllables	Harder Suffixes	Bases or Roots	Feature Points	Words Spelled Correctly
19. ripen									p	en				
20. cellar									ll	ar				
21. pleasure											ure	pleas		
22. fortunate							or				ate	fortun		
23. confident											ent	confid		
24. civilize											ize	civil		
25. opposition											tion	pos		
Totals	/7		/5	/6	/7	/5	/7	/5	/5	/5	/5	/5	/62	/25

Words Their Way Elementary Spelling Inventory Classroom Composite

Teacher _____ School _____ Grade _____ Date _____

SPELLING STAGES → / Students' Names	EMERGENT LATE - EARLY	LETTER NAME-ALPHABETIC EARLY — MIDDLE — LATE			WITHIN WORD PATTERN EARLY — MIDDLE — LATE			SYLLABLES AND AFFIXES EARLY — MIDDLE — LATE				DERIVATIONAL RELATIONS EARLY — MIDDLE			
	Consonants	Short Vowels	Digraphs	Blends	Long Vowels	Other Vowels	Inflected Endings	Syllable Junctures	Unaccented Final Syllables	Harder Suffixes	Bases or Roots	Correct Spelling	Total Rank Order
Possible Points	7	5	6	7	5	7	5	5	5	5	5	25	87
1.													
2.													
3.													
4.													
5.													
6.													
7.													
8.													
9.													
10.													
11.													
12.													
13.													
14.													
15.													
16.													
17.													
18.													
19.													

(continued)

© Macmillan/McGraw-Hill

Words Their Way Elementary Spelling Inventory Classroom Composite

Teacher _____ School _____ Grade _____ Date _____

SPELLING STAGES →	EMERGENT LATE / LETTER NAME-ALPHABETIC EARLY MIDDLE LATE				WITHIN WORD PATTERN EARLY MIDDLE LATE			SYLLABLES AND AFFIXES EARLY MIDDLE LATE			DERIVATIONAL RELATIONS EARLY MIDDLE			
Students' Names	Consonants	Short Vowels	Digraphs	Blends	Long Vowels	Other Vowels	Inflected Endings	Syllable Junctures	Unaccented Final Syllables	Harder Suffixes	Bases or Roots	Correct Spelling	Total Rank Order	
Possible Points	7	5	6	7	5	7	5	5	5	5	5	25	87	
20.														
21.														
22.														
23.														
24.														
25.														
Highlight for Instruction*														

Note: *Highlight students who miss more than 1 on a particular feature; they will benefit from more instruction in that area.

Upper-Level Spelling Inventory (USI)

The Upper-Level Spelling Inventory (USI) can be used in upper elementary. middle, high school, and postsecondary classrooms. The 31 words are ordered by difficulty to sample features of the within word pattern to derivational relations spelling stages. With normally achieving students, you can administer the entire list, but you may stop when students misspell more than eight words and are experiencing noticeable frustration. If any students misspell five of the first eight words, use the ESI to more accurately identify within word pattern features that need instruction.

1. switch — We can switch television channels with a remote control. *switch*
2. smudge — There was a smudge on the mirror from her fingertips. *smudge*
3. trapped — He was trapped in the elevator when the electricity went off. *trapped*
4. scrape — The fall caused her to scrape her knee. *scrape*
5. knotted — The knotted rope would not come undone. *knotted*
6. shaving — He didn't start shaving with a razor until 11th grade. *shaving*
7. squirt — Don't let the ketchup squirt out of the bottle too fast. *squirt*
8. pounce — My cat likes to pounce on her toy mouse. *pounce*
9. scratches — We had to paint over the scratches on the car. *scratches*
10. crater — The crater of the volcano was filled with bubbling lava. *crater*
11. sailor — When he was young. he wanted to go to sea as a sailor. *sailor*
12. village — My Granddad lived in a small seaside village. *village*
13. disloyal — Traitors are disloyal to their country. *disloyal*
14. tunnel — The rockslide closed the tunnel through the mountain. *tunnel*
15. humor — You need a sense of humor to understand his jokes. *humor*
16. confidence — With each winning game, the team's confidence grew. *confidence*

Diagnostic Assessment

Spelling Grades K–6

17.	fortunate	The driver was fortunate to have snow tires on that winter day. *fortunate*
18.	visible	The singer on the stage was visible to everyone. *visible*
19.	circumference	The length of the equator is equal to the circumference of the earth. *circumference*
20.	civilization	We studied the ancient Mayan civilization last year. *civilization*
21.	monarchy	A monarchy is headed by a king or a queen. *monarchy*
22.	dominance	The dominance of the Yankee's baseball team lasted for several years. *dominance*
23.	correspond	Many students correspond through e-mail. *correspond*
24.	illiterate	It is hard to get a job if you are illiterate. *illiterate*
25.	emphasize	I want to emphasize the importance of trying your best. *emphasize*
26.	opposition	The coach said the opposition would give us a tough game. *opposition*
27.	chlorine	My eyes were burning from the chlorine in the swimming pool. *chlorine*
28.	commotion	The audience heard the commotion backstage. *commotion*
29.	medicinal	Cough drops are to be taken for medicinal purposes only. *medicinal*
30.	irresponsible	It is irresponsible not to wear a seat belt. *irresponsible*
31.	succession	The firecrackers went off in rapid succession. *succession*

Words Their Way Upper-Level Spelling Inventory Feature Guide

Student's Name _____ Teacher _____ Grade _____ Date _____

Words Spelled Correctly: ___ /31 *Feature Points:* ___ /68 *Total:* ___ /99 *Spelling Stage:* _____

| SPELLING STAGES → | WITHIN WORD PATTERN | | | SYLLABLES AND AFFIXES | | | DERIVATIONAL RELATIONS | | | Feature Points | Words Spelled Correctly |
| | EARLY | MIDDLE | LATE | EARLY | MIDDLE | LATE | EARLY | MIDDLE | LATE | | |
Features →	Blends and Digraphs	Vowels	Complex Consonants	Inflected Endings and Syllable Juncture	Unaccented Final Syllable	Affixes	Reduced Vowels in Unaccented Syllables	Greek and Latin Elements	Assimilated Prefixes		
1. switch	sw	i	tch								
2. smudge	sm	u	dge								
3. trapped	tr			pped							
4. scrape		a-e	scr								
5. knotted		o	kn	tted							
6. shaving	sh			ving							
7. squirt		ir	squ								
8. pounce		ou	ce								
9. scratches		a	tch	es							
10. crater	cr			t	er						
11. sailor		ai			or						
12. village				ll	age						
13. disloyal		oy			al	dis					
14. tunnel				nn	el						
15. humor				m	or						
16. confidence						con	fid				
17. fortunate					ate			fortun			
Subtotals	/5	/9	/7	/8	/7	/2	/1	/1	/0	/40	/17

(continued)

© Macmillan/McGraw-Hill

Words Their Way Upper-Level Spelling Inventory Feature Guide

Student's Name _____ Teacher _____ Grade _____ Date _____

Words Spelled Correctly: ____/31 Feature Points: ____/68 Total: ____/99 Spelling Stage: _____

SPELLING STAGES → / Features →	WITHIN WORD PATTERN Blends and Digraphs (EARLY)	Vowels (MIDDLE)	Complex Consonants (LATE)	SYLLABLES AND AFFIXES Inflected Endings and Syllable Juncture (EARLY)	Unaccented Final Syllable (MIDDLE)	Affixes (LATE)	DERIVATIONAL RELATIONS Reduced Vowels in Unaccented Syllables (EARLY)	Greek and Latin Elements (MIDDLE)	Assimilated Prefixes (LATE)	Feature Points	Words Spelled Correctly
18. visible						ible		vis			
19. circumference						ence		circum			
20. civilization							liz	civil			
21. monarchy								arch			
22. dominance						ance	min				
23. correspond							res		rr		
24. illiterate					ate				ll		
25. emphasize						size	pha				
26. opposition							pos		pp		
27. chlorine						ine		chlor			
28. commotion						tion			mm		
29. medicinal					al			medic			
30. irresponsible						ible	res		rr		
31. succession						sion			cc		
Subtotals	/0	/0	/0	/0	/2	/8	/6	/6	/6	/28	/14
Totals*	/5	/9	/7	/8	/9	/10	/7	/7	/6	/68	/31

Spelling Grades K–6

Words Their Way Upper-Level Spelling Inventory Classroom Composite

Teacher _____ School _____ Grade _____ Date _____

SPELLING STAGES → Students' Names	WITHIN WORD PATTERN			SYLLABLES AND AFFIXES			DERIVATIONAL RELATIONS			
	EARLY MIDDLE LATE			EARLY MIDDLE LATE			EARLY MIDDLE LATE			
	Blends and Digraphs	Vowels	Complex Consonants	Inflected Endings and Syllable Junctures	Unaccented Final Syllables	Affixes	Reduced Vowels in Unaccented Syllables	Greek and Latin Elements	Assimilated Prefixes	Total Rank Order
Possible Points	5	9	7	8	9	10	7	7	6	99
1.										
2.										
3.										
4.										
5.										
6.										
7.										
8.										
9.										
10.										
11.										
12.										
13.										
14.										
15.										
16.										
17.										
18.										
19.										

(continued)

Spelling Grades K-6

© Macmillan/McGraw-Hill

Words Their Way Upper-Level Spelling Inventory Classroom Composite

Teacher _____ School _____ Grade _____ Date _____

SPELLING STAGES → Students' Names	WITHIN WORD PATTERN EARLY MIDDLE LATE			SYLLABLES AND AFFIXES EARLY MIDDLE LATE			DERIVATIONAL RELATIONS EARLY MIDDLE LATE			
	Blends and Digraphs	Vowels	Complex Consonants	Inflected Endings and Syllable Junctures	Unaccented Final Syllables	Affixes	Reduced Vowels in Unaccented Syllables	Greek and Latin Elements	Assimilated Prefixes	Total Rank Order
Possible Points	5	9	7	8	9	10	7	7	6	99
20.										
21.										
22.										
23.										
24.										
25.										
26.										
27.										
Highlight for Instruction*										

*Highlight students who miss more than 1 on a particular feature if tried total is between 5 and 8. Highlight those who miss more than 2 if the total is between 9 and 10.

K–6 Diagnostic Assessment

Vocabulary

- ## Critchlow Verbal Language Scales

Critchlow Verbal Language Scales

SKILL ASSESSED
Vocabulary

Grade Level

K–6

Language

• English

Grouping

Individual

Approximate Testing Time

15 Minutes

Materials

• English Record Form (p. 3)

Source

From *Dos Amigos Verbal Language Scales* by Donald E. Critchlow.

WHAT   The *Critchlow Verbal Language Scales* assess a student's vocabulary in English. Vocabulary is assessed by asking a student to say the "opposite" of a series of words spoken by the examiner. The words on this assessment are arranged in increasing order of difficulty. The scale contains 75 English stimulus words.

WHY   As students progress through the grades, they build larger and larger vocabularies. A more advanced vocabulary enables students to better comprehend what they read and hear as well as to better express their thoughts. Measuring vocabulary provides an index of what a student has learned and how well equipped the student is for future learning.

HOW   Before beginning the test, determine that the student understands what an opposite is and can demonstrate this knowledge. For example say: "If it is not daytime, it is _____" or "If a child is not a boy, it is a _____" to help establish the concept of opposite.

Explain to the student that you are going to say a word and he or she is to respond with the opposite of that word. Begin with item 1 for all students, and discontinue testing after the child misses five consecutive words or completes the scale. Do not give credit for a response that is not listed.

Note that alternatives are sometimes provided for a stimulus or acceptable response. For example, the response to *absent* is listed as *present-here,* indicating that either response is correct.

© Macmillan/McGraw-Hill

Vocabulary Grades K–6

WHAT IT MEANS   Count the number correct and refer to the scoring criteria below to identify the approximate vocabulary grade level. For students who score below their current grade level, provide direct instruction in specific vocabulary needed for school success.

Number Correct English	Vocabulary Grade Level
1–8	Grade K and below
9–12	Grade 1
13–17	Grade 2
18–21	Grade 3
22–26	Grade 4
27–30	Grade 5
31–34 and above	Grade 6 and above

WHAT'S NEXT?   For students with limited vocabulary, more intense support in developing other underlying reading skills may be warranted. Further testing of fluency, phonics, or phoneme segmentation ability may be indicated.

Critchlow Verbal Language Scale

Name: _____ Grade: _____ Date: _____

Directions: Ask the student to say the opposite of each word. Discontinue testing after five consecutive errors.

	STIMULUS	RESPONSE		STIMULUS	RESPONSE
_____	1. boy	girl	_____	39. multiply	divide
_____	2. up	down	_____	40. friend	enemy
_____	3. front	back	_____	41. difficult	easy
_____	4. hot	cold	_____	42. narrow	wide
_____	5. brother	sister	_____	43. wild	tame
_____	6. dirty	clean	_____	44. dangerous	safe
_____	7. wet	dry	_____	45. entrance	exit
_____	8. crooked	straight	_____	46. sharp	dull
_____	9. young	old	_____	47. imprisoned	free
_____	10. off	on	_____	48. falsehood	truth
_____	11. shut	open	_____	49. public	private
_____	12. noisy	quiet	_____	50. costly	cheap
_____	13. dead	alive	_____	51. lengthen	shorten
_____	14. early	late	_____	52. succeed	fail
_____	15. empty	full	_____	53. victory	defeat
_____	16. near	far	_____	54. stale	fresh
_____	17. come	go	_____	55. timid	bold-brave
_____	18. north	south	_____	56. maximum	minimum
_____	19. lost	found	_____	57. unite	separate
_____	20. pretty	ugly-homely	_____	58. profit	loss
_____	21. sick	well	_____	59. complex	simple
_____	22. sour	sweet	_____	60. create	destroy
_____	23. add	subtract	_____	61. vertical	horizontal
_____	24. daughter	son	_____	62. former	latter
_____	25. remember	forget	_____	63. bless	curse
_____	26. false	true	_____	64. loiter	hurry
_____	27. love	hate	_____	65. discord	harmony
_____	28. heavy	light	_____	66. gradual	sudden
_____	29. tight	loose	_____	67. diminish	increase
_____	30. after	before	_____	68. naive	sophisticated
_____	31. laugh	cry	_____	69. superfluous	necessary
_____	32. smooth	rough	_____	70. asset	liability
_____	33. absent	present-here	_____	71. tentative	permanent
_____	34. strong	weak	_____	72. clergy	laity
_____	35. evening	morning	_____	73. corpulent	slender
_____	36. raw	cooked	_____	74. epilogue	prologue
_____	37. begin	end-stop	_____	75. autocracy	democracy
_____	38. same	different			

Score: _____ /75

© Macmillan/McGraw-Hill

Diagnostic Assessment

K–6 Diagnostic
Assessment

Reading Comprehension

- **Comprehension Tests Grades K–6**
- **Metacomprehension Strategy Index**
- **McLeod Assessment of Reading Comprehension**

Comprehension Tests K-6

▶ **WHAT** The *Comprehension Tests* assess overall reading comprehension and grade-level reading proficiency. Students read a series of passages that get progressively harder and answer accompanying comprehension questions. There is one set of passages and questions for each grade level. It is useful to test frequently in the elementary and middle school grades.

▶ **WHY** Comprehension is the ultimate goal of reading. This assessment requires students to accurately decode words, to apply their knowledge of vocabulary, and to use critical reading strategies that aid in the literal and inferential comprehension of what is read. When administered to everyone in a class, the assessment serves as a valuable screening for identifying students who may have reading difficulties and who may benefit from additional assessment that focuses on specific skills underlying reading. It can also be used to place students in appropriate-leveled materials to work on critical prerequisite skills and to build overall reading fluency. Since the goal of all instruction is access to core, grade-level content and reading materials, students should only use lower-level materials as needed to work on targeted skills. They should also have exposure to grade-level text and receive ample preteaching and reteaching during small group instructional periods to access this material.

▶ **HOW** Make booklets for students by copying the passages and questions in grade-level order. Begin with passages two grade levels below the students' current grade and end two grade levels above the current grade (if applicable). For example, a grade 4 student would receive a booklet containing grades 2–6 passages and questions. Distribute the booklets to the students.

Explain to students that this test will help you find the best reading level for them so that they can enjoy reading and build their reading skills. Make sure students are sitting in a comfortable setting with minimal distractions, and encourage them to do their best on the test.

In order to administer the test efficiently and make the directions understandable, you should be familiar with the directions and the test items before the test is given. During the administration, monitor students closely to make sure that each student is following the directions, is on the correct item, and is marking the test form correctly.

▶ **WHAT IT MEANS** The assessment can be scored using the Answer Key at the end of this section (page 295). It lists the correct response for each question. Mark each incorrect item on the student's test, and record the number of correct items. To find the percentage for each score, use the Scoring Chart at the end of this section (page 296).

If students achieve a score of 80%–90%, then they should receive instruction on that grade level. If students receive a score below 80%, then administer additional assessments to determine specific skill needs. These students may need targeted skills-based instruction during small group time to build mastery of prerequisite skills. These students may struggle with grade-level text and will need ample preteaching and reteaching of core content. If students score higher than 90%, monitor their progress in the weeks following the assessment. You might consider providing advanced, or beyond-level, instruction and practice to accelerate their reading growth and enrich the grade-level activities provided.

Reading Comprehension Grades K–6

Directions:

Give the child a copy of the Comprehension section of the test. Read the story and the questions aloud. The child will answer the question by marking the answers.

Now I am going to read you a story. Listen to the story. Then I will ask you some questions. Here is the story.

The Amazing Fish

One day, a fisherman caught an amazing fish with his fishing pole. The fish asked to be let go. "I will grant you three wishes if you let me go," the fish said.

"Very well, said the fisherman. "I wish to be a king."

The fish granted the fisherman's first wish, but the fisherman was not happy.

"I wish for a castle," said the fisherman. So the fish granted the fisherman's second wish, but the fisherman was not happy.

"I wish for a bigger castle," said the fisherman. "I want one that reaches up to the sun!"

"That is not possible," said the fish. "Wish again."

The fisherman became very angry and stomped his foot. "Oh, how I wish I had never met you!" he screamed.

So the fish granted the fisherman's last wish. In an instant, the fisherman was no longer a king with a castle. He was a fisherman fishing in the sea.

Diagnostic Assessment

Now I will read some questions.

Have the child look at page 4.

1. *Point to the star. Look at the pictures. Which picture shows what the fisherman wished for first? Circle the picture.*

2. *Point to the sun. Look at the pictures. Which picture shows what happened to the fisherman at the end of the story? Circle the picture.*

Have the child look at page 5.

3. *Point to the circle. Look at the pictures. Which picture shows what the fisherman wanted his castle to reach up to? Circle the picture.*

4. *Point to the triangle. Look at the pictures. Which picture shows something the fisherman used to catch fish? Circle the picture.*

Have the child look at page 6.

5. *Point to the moon. Look at the pictures. Which picture shows something that could __not__ really happen? Circle the picture.*

6. *Point to the square. Look at the pictures. Which picture shows what will happen to the fisherman next? Circle the picture.*

Comprehension

1.

2.

Diagnostic Assessment

Reading Comprehension Grades K-6

Comprehension

3.

4.

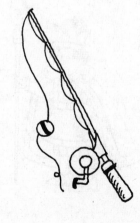 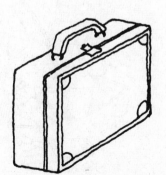 

Reading Comprehension Grades K–6

Comprehension

5.

6.

Diagnostic Assessment

Reading Comprehension Grades K–6

Directions:

Have children turn to the Comprehension section of the test. There are two reading passages in this section. You will read the passages and the questions aloud. Children will answer the questions by marking pictures.

Now I am going to read you some stories. Listen to the first story. Then I will ask you some questions. Here is the story.

Have you ever seen a real bear? Most bears live in the mountains or the forest. Bears like to eat many different foods. They eat lots of nuts and berries. Some bears catch and eat fish from the rivers. One of the bear's favorite foods is honey, which is made by bees. The bear finds a beehive and takes the honey.

All through the summer, bears eat a lot and get very big. When fall comes, the weather gets colder. When the leaves fall off the trees, the bear knows that winter will come soon. The bear finds a good place to go for winter, such as a cave or a hole in the ground. The bear climbs in and goes to sleep for the winter. In the spring, the bear will wake up and start eating again.

Now I will read some questions.

1. *Point to the star at the top of the page. Look at the pictures. What is the story mostly about? Fill in the circle under the picture that shows what the story is mostly about.*

2. *Point to the moon. Which picture shows where a bear gets honey? Fill in the circle under the picture that shows where the bear gets honey.*

3. *Point to the sun. Which picture shows how the bear knows when winter is coming? Fill in the circle under the picture that shows how the bear knows that winter is coming.*

4. *Point to the heart. Which picture shows where a bear likes to sleep for the winter? Fill in the circle under the picture that shows where a bear likes to sleep.*

Have children turn to the next page.

Now I am going to read another story. Listen carefully. Here is the story.

Working with Mom

Maya and Sam were excited about spending the day at the flower shop with their moms. Maya and Sam were best friends. Their families lived in the same apartment building, and their moms worked together in the same flower shop.

On Saturday morning, the four of them rode the bus together to the shop. When they got there, Maya's mom opened the door with a key. When the door opened, a little bell jingled.

"That bell will let us know when someone comes to buy something," said Sam's mom.

A minute later, the bell jingled. The first customer walked in.

"Hello, may I help you?" asked Maya's mom.

The man told them he would like a bouquet of fresh flowers.

"We'll make that for you, and it will be beautiful," said Maya's mom. "We have lots of help today."

Sam and Maya helped their moms choose the flowers. Sam's mom snipped the stems and put everything into a vase. "It's so pretty," said Maya.

The man was happy, too. "I think you should let these two come to work with you more often!" he said, smiling at Maya and Sam.

Maya and Sam were happy with the work they had done.

Now I will read some questions.

5. *Point to the star at the top of the page. Look at the pictures. Which picture shows what this story is mostly about? Fill in the circle under the picture.*

6. *Point to the moon. Which picture shows how Maya and Sam and their moms got to work? Fill in the circle under the picture that shows how they got to work.*

7. *Point to the sun. Which picture shows something that happens at the beginning of the story? Fill in the circle under the picture that shows something that happens at the beginning of the story.*

8. *Point to the heart. Which picture best shows how the two families feel about each other? Fill in the circle under the picture that best shows how the two families feel about each other.*

Reading Comprehension Grades K–6

Comprehension

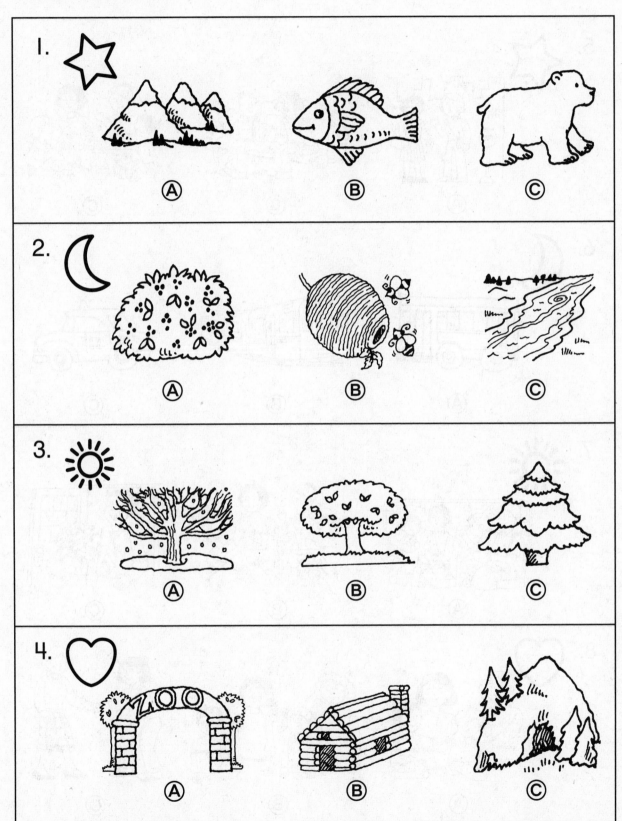

1. A B C

2. A B C

3. A B C

4. A B C

Comprehension

Diagnostic Assessment

Reading Comprehension Grades K–6

Directions:

Have children turn to the Comprehension section of the test. Then give them these directions.

This part of the test has two reading passages and 10 questions. Read each passage and answer the questions that follow. Mark your answers.

Have children read the passages and answer questions 1–10 independently.

Comprehension

Read this story about a girl named Kate. Then answer questions 1–5. Mark your answers.

On the Train

Kate could hardly keep her eyes open. She was trying to read. She was sitting on the train beside her brother Jed. Mom and Dad were sitting one row behind them. They were all going to Baltimore to visit Grandpa. Kate picked up her book again. Her eyes still would not stay open. She was so tired that she fell asleep. Soon she began to dream. She dreamed that a funny thing happened. She looked at the seat

© Macmillan/McGraw-Hill

next to her. Jed was not there. Instead, a bear was sitting in the seat. It was a trained bear from a circus.

"How did you get here?" asked Kate. "Who are you, and where's Jed?"

"My name is Belle," said the bear. "Jed and I traded places. He is working at the circus now. I am going to Baltimore with you."

"Oh, but I miss my brother," said Kate. "We must bring him back."

"That's okay with me," said Belle. "I miss my friends at the circus, too."

Kate and Belle made the train stop. Then they got off the train. They went to the circus. Jed was there. He was trying to ride a bear's funny bike.

"Boy, am I glad to see you," said Jed. "Being in the circus is not much fun. Besides, I can't ride this silly bike."

"That bike is not silly," said Belle. "That is my bike."

Belle climbed on the bike. She began to ride around. She waved at all her friends. She seemed happy to be back at the circus. Kate looked at Jed and said, "Let's go back to the train."

"You bet!" said Jed.

Just then, Kate woke up. She looked at the seat beside her. Jed was there reading his book.

"What a funny dream," thought Kate.

Diagnostic Assessment

Reading Comprehension Grades K-6

1. What happened to Kate in this story?
   Ⓐ She got a job at the circus.
   Ⓑ She fell off a bike.
   Ⓒ She changed her name to Belle.
   Ⓓ She had a dream.

2. Why were Jed and Kate going to Baltimore?
   Ⓐ They were going to visit Grandpa.
   Ⓑ They wanted to join a circus.
   Ⓒ They were going to see Belle.
   Ⓓ They wanted to visit Mom and Dad.

3. How did Kate feel when she saw Belle in the seat beside her?
   Ⓐ upset
   Ⓑ glad
   Ⓒ angry
   Ⓓ surprised

4. What can you tell about Belle?

   Ⓐ She works in a circus.

   Ⓑ She wants to go to Baltimore.

   Ⓒ She knows Grandpa.

   Ⓓ She does not like trains.

5. What happened last?

   Ⓐ Belle got off the train.

   Ⓑ Kate woke up.

   Ⓒ Jed went to the circus.

   Ⓓ Kate got on the train.

Comprehension

Read this passage about a pony. Then answer
questions 6–10. Mark your answers.

Gentle Friends

Have you ever heard of a Shetland pony? Ponies are very small horses. The Shetland pony is the smallest horse of all. The largest Shetland pony is less than four feet tall. The smallest may only grow to about two feet tall. That is a lot shorter than a boy or girl in second grade!

Shetland ponies come from the Shetland Islands near Scotland. These islands can be very cold. Shetland ponies have very long hair. Their hair can have many shades of color. Most of the ponies have patches of black and white.

Shetland ponies are very strong. Long ago, they worked in coal mines. Coal mines are places where people dig coal out of the ground. The ponies were small enough to go into the mines. They were also strong enough to pull wagons filled with coal.

Children love Shetland ponies because they are very calm. They never get upset. Did you ever go on a pony ride? If you did, you most likely rode a Shetland pony.

Today, some Shetland ponies work on farms. Most of them are pets or horses kept for show. Do you think you would like to have a Shetland pony?

6. What is this passage MOSTLY about?

   Ⓐ coal mines

   Ⓑ farms in Scotland

   Ⓒ Shetland ponies

   Ⓓ children and their pets

7. Why were Shetland ponies good for working in coal mines?

   Ⓐ They are small and strong.

   Ⓑ They are easy to train.

   Ⓒ They can see in the dark.

   Ⓓ They can smell coal.

8. Shetland ponies probably have long hair to

   Ⓐ look nice.

   Ⓑ keep warm.

   Ⓒ change colors.

   Ⓓ stay clean.

9. From this passage, what can you tell about coal mines?

   Ⓐ They have lots of light.

   Ⓑ They do not have much room.

   Ⓒ They are very clean.

   Ⓓ They do not have any coal left.

10. Shetland ponies are used to give pony rides because they

    Ⓐ come from islands near Scotland.

    Ⓑ have long hair.

    Ⓒ may be almost any color.

    Ⓓ are very gentle.

Comprehension

Read each passage and answer the questions that follow.

Friends

One day, a young bear, a beaver, and a raccoon were playing hide-and-seek in the woods. A small brown rabbit came hopping down the path and asked to play.

"Sure," said the bear, "you can join us."

"Let's play catch," said Rabbit.

"Oh, but we're playing hide-and-seek," said Beaver. Bear looked at Beaver. "All right, we'll play catch," Beaver agreed.

The animals had not played catch for very long before Rabbit demanded, "Let's play leapfrog!"

"We're playing catch," said Raccoon.

"I'm tired of playing catch," moaned Rabbit.

"Okay," said Bear, who was a bit upset but wanted to be nice to their new friend. The animals switched to leapfrog, but not for long. Rabbit soon complained, "I'm sick of this game. Let's play tag!"

Beaver had had enough. He said, "I have to go home now." Then he turned and walked away.

"I think I hear my mom calling. See you later!" said Bear, who headed toward the hills.

"I have to go, too," said Raccoon.

Rabbit was left all alone.

Reading Comprehension Grades K–6

1. Where does this story take place?
   - Ⓐ at school
   - Ⓑ on a playground
   - Ⓒ by a pond
   - Ⓓ in the woods

2. What were the animals playing first?
   - Ⓐ hide-and-seek
   - Ⓑ catch
   - Ⓒ leapfrog
   - Ⓓ tag

3. Which word BEST describes Rabbit?
   - Ⓐ funny
   - Ⓑ selfish
   - Ⓒ caring
   - Ⓓ worried

4. Compare how the animals felt before Rabbit came and at the end of the story.
   - Ⓐ First they were happy, then they were upset.
   - Ⓑ First they were sad, then they were happy.
   - Ⓒ First they were bored, then they were afraid.
   - Ⓓ First they were angry, then they were sad.

5. Why did Bear say, "I think I hear my mom calling. See you later!" when Rabbit said he wanted to play tag?
   - Ⓐ Bear really did hear his mom calling him for dinner.
   - Ⓑ Bear was tired of switching games for Rabbit and lost interest in playing.
   - Ⓒ Bear was going to secretly play a game with Rabbit after Beaver went home.
   - Ⓓ Bear was going to go to Beaver's house.

Protecting the Gorillas

Forty years ago, there were not many gorillas left in Africa. Wild gorillas were being killed by hunters, and they would soon all be gone. A woman named Dian Fossey helped change that.

Dr. Fossey was from California. She was born in 1932. She loved working with animals, so she went to Africa in 1963. There she met a scientist named Dr. Louis Leakey. Dr. Leakey was studying great apes. Dian Fossey began learning about apes, too. She studied mountain gorillas.

Dr. Fossey spent some time studying gorillas in Zaire and in Rwanda. She wanted to prove that gorillas could be gentle animals, and could become friends with people. In 1967, she built a camp in the mountains called Karisoke. She lived there for a long time.

In 1970, a gorilla named Peanuts reached out and touched Dr. Fossey's hand. It was the first time a gorilla had ever touched a person in a friendly way. Before long, the wild gorillas all came to trust Dr. Fossey. This helped her understand more about the way gorillas behave. She was the first person to be this close with gorillas.

Dr. Fossey spent the rest of her life working to protect mountain gorillas. Her favorite gorilla, Digit, was killed by hunters. Dr. Fossey told the world about Digit in a story she wrote for *National Geographic* magazine. Many people read Dr. Fossey's story and wanted to send money to help protect the gorillas.

A few years later, Dr. Fossey wrote a book called *Gorillas in the Mist*, and it was made into a movie. This story of her work helped people around the world understand more about gorillas. By the early 1980's, there were about 250 wild gorillas in Africa. Dr. Fossey died in 1985, but her work lives on. Today, there are many more wild mountain gorillas. Scientists still work at Karisoke to protect the gorillas, and—thanks to Dr. Fossey—we know more about the great apes than ever before.

6. What is the MAIN idea of this passage?
   Ⓐ A gorilla named Peanuts touched Dr. Fossey's hand.
   Ⓑ Dian Fossey spent much of her life studying and protecting gorillas.
   Ⓒ Most of the gorillas in Africa were killed by hunters.
   Ⓓ Dian Fossey was born in California in 1932 and went to Africa in 1963.

7. Dian Fossey went to Africa because she wanted to
   Ⓐ work with animals.
   Ⓑ meet with Dr. Leakey.
   Ⓒ build a camp.
   Ⓓ write a magazine story.

8. Which detail shows that gorillas could be gentle and friendly to people?

    Ⓐ Dr. Fossey built a camp near the gorillas.

    Ⓑ She wrote an article about a gorilla.

    Ⓒ Peanuts touched Dr. Fossey's hand.

    Ⓓ Scientists still work at Karisoke today.

9. Why did people give money to Dr. Fossey to help the gorillas?

    Ⓐ Dr. Leakey asked people to send money.

    Ⓑ They wanted her to make a movie about gorillas.

    Ⓒ She had built a camp in the mountains.

    Ⓓ They read about her work in a magazine.

10. Why did Dr. Fossey want to live in the mountains?

    Ⓐ She loved the outdoors.

    Ⓑ She wanted to live near the gorillas.

    Ⓒ She was bored living in the city.

    Ⓓ She wanted to learn how to hunt.

Comprehension

Read each passage and answer the questions that follow.

The Animal Hunt

Yesterday was my brother Ben's fifth birthday party. As usual, since I'm the older sister, I had to help out. Mom said, "Leslie, five busy boys need to be watched carefully. You can't let them out of your sight for a minute or you'll lose one." Then she put me in charge of the games.

Since I didn't want to lose anybody, I planned only one game for the boys to play outside. Ben loved animals and looking for hidden things. So I took ten of his plastic toy animals and hid them in the vacant lot next to our apartment building. By the time I was done, there were three bears, two snakes, three monkeys, one giraffe, and one lion hidden all over the lot.

When Ben's four friends arrived for the party, I could hardly believe how noisy and excited they were. Mom said, "Leslie, I'm going to cook the pizza. You can play your game outside with the boys. Then bring them in to eat."

"Okay, Ben," I announced. "It's time to go on a safari. The boy who finds the most animals will win a prize. I have hidden ten toy animals in the empty lot. Meet me out front in one minute." The boys raced down the stairs. Then they lined up on the sidewalk ready to begin.

"On your mark, get set, go!" I cried, pointing them all toward the lot next door.

Ben and his friends tore around the lot looking under the rocks and in the grass. They shrieked and laughed as they discovered eight of the animals. Only the giraffe and a snake were still hidden. Then I noticed Chris, Ben's best friend. He was waving a snake around calling, "I found the snake!"

As I looked more closely, I knew it was not one of the thick, black, rubber snakes that I had hidden. This snake was long and thin. "Drop it, drop it!" I screamed. I had no idea whether this kind of snake was dangerous or not, but I was not going to take any chances.

Chris threw the snake up into the air. I ran over just in time to see its tail disappear under a rock. Suddenly my heart was pumping wildly. "Chris, that snake was alive! I never hid that snake. Did it bite you?" I questioned him and carefully examined his hands and arms.

He replied calmly. "No, I just picked it up and then threw it when you told me to." He looked at me and asked, "Will it count toward the prize?"

"Yes, of course," I answered, chuckling in spite of myself. Then I warned the boys, "Be careful not to pick up anything that is alive. The toy snakes are black and thick."

The rest of the game passed in slow motion for me. The boys dashed around and poked in the dirt. As soon as they uncovered the last two animals, I hurried them upstairs before anything else could happen.

Everyone agreed that Chris was the winner. He found three toy animals and one living snake!

1. Where do Ben and his sister live?
   Ⓐ on a farm
   Ⓑ in the woods
   Ⓒ in an apartment building
   Ⓓ beside a zoo

2. Which word *best* describes Ben's sister Leslie?
   Ⓐ helpful
   Ⓑ silly
   Ⓒ selfish
   Ⓓ brave

3. What happened just after Chris threw the snake into the air?
   Ⓐ Leslie made the boys go inside.
   Ⓑ Ben's mom made a pizza.
   Ⓒ The boys lined up on the sidewalk.
   Ⓓ The snake went under a rock.

4. Leslie was probably upset by the snake because she
   Ⓐ did not want one of the boys to get lost.
   Ⓑ forgot where she put it.
   Ⓒ was worried that the snake would bite Chris.
   Ⓓ did not like toy snakes.

5. Why did the rest of the game go in slow motion for Leslie?
   Ⓐ Leslie was still in shock that Chris picked up a snake.
   Ⓑ Leslie was in a trance.
   Ⓒ Leslie couldn't wait for the party to begin.
   Ⓓ Leslie was bored.

6. How was Leslie *different* after Chris picked up the snake?
   Ⓐ She did not want to help with the party anymore.
   Ⓑ She was worried about the boys.
   Ⓒ She felt more confident about herself.
   Ⓓ She thought that time went by too fast.

7. By the end of the day, what did Leslie *most likely* learn?
   Ⓐ Children like to eat pizza.
   Ⓑ Birthday parties are fun.
   Ⓒ Children do need to be watched carefully.
   Ⓓ Most birthday parties are peaceful and quiet.

Dr. Drew: A Great American

Every year, about 8 million Americans give blood to help others. This blood is saved in places called "blood banks." Then it is used to help people who are injured or become sick. How can blood be saved in a bank until it is needed? The work of an African-American man named Charles Drew made it possible.

Charles Richard Drew was born in Washington, D.C., in 1904. In school, Charles got good grades, and he was always good in sports. In high school, he was named best all-around athlete. He did especially well in track and football. He probably could have become a professional athlete, but he decided not to. When Charles was 15 years old, his sister died of tuberculosis. That is a disease of the lungs. After experiencing his sister's illness, Charles decided to become a doctor. He first attended college in Baltimore and then went to McGill University in Montreal, Canada, to become a doctor. There he met Dr. John Beattie, who was one of his teachers. Charles Drew became interested in Dr. Beattie's work with blood. He soon began reading all he could about blood. He and Dr. Beattie became good friends. They worked together until Charles finished school.

Dr. Drew continued to study blood. In 1938, he wrote an important paper called "Banked Blood." It was about the best ways to save blood in a blood bank. Drew discovered new ways to store large amounts of blood—and just in time! Drew made his discovery just when the fighting of World War II began. A lot of blood was needed to save wounded soldiers, and Dr. Drew was the man to collect it. In 1941, he became the head of the American Red Cross Blood Bank in New York. He was in charge of the blood that would be used for the U.S. Army and Navy.

Dr. Charles Drew and his work probably saved millions of lives during the war and in the years since then. He was a remarkable man. To honor Dr. Drew, the U.S. Postal Service issued a stamp with his picture on it in 1981. The stamp was part of a special series called "Great Americans."

8. What is this passage *mostly* about?
   Ⓐ a series of stamps called "Great Americans"
   Ⓑ Dr. Charles Drew and his work with blood
   Ⓒ why Dr. Drew went to school in Canada
   Ⓓ how the United States got into World War II

9. Which detail supports the idea that Charles Drew was a "Great American"?
   Ⓐ He grew up in Washington, D.C.
   Ⓑ He went to McGill University in Canada.
   Ⓒ His discovery saved millions of lives.
   Ⓓ He wrote a paper called "Banked Blood."

10. What did Charles Drew do just after high school?
    Ⓐ He became a professional athlete.
    Ⓑ He wrote a paper about blood.
    Ⓒ He joined the U.S. Army.
    Ⓓ He went to college.

11. Charles Drew decided to become a doctor because
    Ⓐ he was not very good at sports.
    Ⓑ he lost his sister to a disease.
    Ⓒ he always got good grades in school.
    Ⓓ he knew that people needed him.

12. The purpose of this passage is to
    Ⓐ persuade people to give blood.
    Ⓑ compare Charles Drew with other doctors.
    Ⓒ give information about Charles Drew.
    Ⓓ tell an entertaining story about Charles Drew.

13. Before Dr. Charles Drew made his discovery, people did not know how to
    Ⓐ store large amounts of blood.
    Ⓑ become professional athletes.
    Ⓒ recognize different kinds of disease.
    Ⓓ save soldiers who were wounded.

14. Which sentence states a fact?
    Ⓐ Charles was always a good student.
    Ⓑ Charles was always good in sports.
    Ⓒ Charles excelled in track and football.
    Ⓓ Charles's sister died of tuberculosis.

15. Which sentence states an opinion?
    Ⓐ Charles decided to become a doctor.
    Ⓑ Charles went to college in Baltimore, Maryland.
    Ⓒ Dr. Drew was a remarkable man.
    Ⓓ The U.S. Postal Service issued a stamp to honor Charles.

16. What did Dr. Drew do just after World War II began?
    Ⓐ He became a doctor.
    Ⓑ He went to McGill University.
    Ⓒ He wrote a paper called "Banked Blood."
    Ⓓ He became the head of the American Red Cross Blood Bank.

Comprehension

Read each passage and answer the questions that follow.

The Lesson

Last fall, a new kid moved to town. His name was Prescott Howard. As if his name weren't formal enough, he also wore a shirt and tie to school every day. When he spoke, he used the kind of language you would use if you were writing a paper for school. He never participated when we played at recess or after school, even though we always invited him to play. He just hung around and watched with his hands in his pockets.

One day after school, Billy, Marta, Jamal, and I were playing ball at the park. Toby, my dog, was tearing back and forth, barking frantically and trying to catch the ball. Pretty soon there was Prescott, sitting on a bench and watching. We ignored him and kept playing. None of us noticed that Toby had disappeared.

Jamal had just scooped up a tough ground ball when we heard brakes squeal. There was a sharp yelp and then the sound of someone driving away fast. I ran toward the street, but when I got there, Prescott was already kneeling by Toby, talking softly to him. Then I saw the most horrible thing. A bone was sticking out of Toby's back leg. I knelt by his head and put out my hand.

"Don't, Betsy," Prescott said sharply. "He won't recognize you right now, and he might bite you. Give me your jacket." Prescott put his hands underneath Toby and slid him onto the jacket. He was so gentle that Toby barely flinched. Prescott flagged down Ms. Ortega, who happened to be driving by, and asked me, "Who's your vet?"

"Dr. Swanson, on Third Street," I said. Prescott opened the car door and asked Ms. Ortega to take us to Third Street.

Toby didn't look good at all. His tongue was hanging out of his mouth and his eyes were glazed. "Will he be okay?" I blurted out.

"Should be," Prescott said calmly, "if your vet is any good." We pulled up in front of Dr. Swanson's office, and Prescott thanked Ms. Ortega. Dr. Swanson rushed Toby into surgery while Prescott and I sat in the waiting room.

"How'd you learn to take care of animals like that?" I asked.

"My mom's a vet," he said. "I used to help her out."

"Well, where's your mom now?"

"She's sick. She had to go to a clinic far away and my dad went with her, so I came to live with my grandmother for a while. Dad grew up in this town."

I didn't know what to say. I felt awkward and awful. Finally I said stupidly, "I guess you ruined your clothes." There was oil from the road on his pants and a bloodstain on his white shirt.

"I know, isn't it great?" Prescott said happily. I stared at him like he was crazy, and finally he sighed and said, "Grams is nice, but she's old-fashioned. She thinks I should wear a shirt and tie to school. Every afternoon we have tea, and dinner is formal, too. She says I don't speak 'correctly.'" He paused, then added, "Dad asked me to do whatever she asked, and I don't want to let him down."

Boy, had I been wrong about this kid! Just then Dr. Swanson came out. "Betsy, Toby will be fine when his leg heals," he said. "Thank your friend here for knowing what to do and getting Toby here before he really went into shock."

I looked at Prescott, who was smiling widely. On the way out I said, "Maybe we could try to explain to your grandmother about clothes, and, uh . . . your name's okay and all, but it's kind of formal."

"My mom calls me Scotty," he said shyly.

"Then come on, Scotty," I said, "we've got to go tell everyone Toby's going to be all right." I clapped him on the shoulder. "And, hey, Scotty, why don't you lose the tie, just for today?"

He pulled off his tie and stuffed it in his pocket. "Race you to your house," he said, and took off. He was actually pretty fast, but he had on dress shoes, so I beat him.

1. Where were the kids at the beginning of this story?
    Ⓐ in school   Ⓒ on the playground
    Ⓑ at the park   Ⓓ at the vet's office

2. According to Betsy, what was Prescott's problem at the beginning?
    Ⓐ He did not like dogs.   Ⓒ He never played with the other kids.
    Ⓑ He could not run very fast. Ⓓ He was living with his grandmother.

© Macmillan/McGraw-Hill

3. What happened just after Prescott came to watch Betsy and her friends play ball?
   Ⓐ Betsy's dog got hit by a car.
   Ⓑ Prescott flagged down Ms. Ortega.
   Ⓒ Betsy and Scotty raced each other to Betsy's house.
   Ⓓ Prescott took off his tie.

4. Which word *best* describes Prescott's manner with animals?
   Ⓐ silly
   Ⓑ timid
   Ⓒ gentle
   Ⓓ rough

5. Prescott flagged down Ms. Ortega because he
   Ⓐ thought Ms. Ortega had hit Toby.
   Ⓑ needed to take Toby to a vet.
   Ⓒ wanted Ms. Ortega to call the police.
   Ⓓ needed a ride home.

6. How was Prescott *different* from the other kids at first?
   Ⓐ He was a better ball player.
   Ⓑ He was much older.
   Ⓒ He was a better student.
   Ⓓ He was more formal.

7. From this experience, Betsy probably learned that
   Ⓐ everybody likes to play baseball.
   Ⓑ dogs should not be allowed in the park.
   Ⓒ she should not judge people so quickly.
   Ⓓ you can't count on anyone but yourself.

From Ostrich to Kiwi

Cassowary, emu, ostrich, kiwi. What are these strange words? They are all names of birds that cannot fly. While these flightless birds are alike in some ways, there are important differences among these odd creatures.

The ostrich is the largest living bird. It may weigh over 300 pounds and stand up to ten feet tall. Its very long neck, small head, and long, thin legs give it an awkward appearance. The ostrich has beautiful, soft plumage, or feathers. It grazes on the African plains. The ostrich can run up to 35 miles an hour. It can also defend itself with its two large, clawed toes.

The Australian emu looks much like an ostrich but is smaller. It weighs about 120 pounds and stands six feet tall. It can run up to 30 miles an hour and is a good swimmer. The plumage of the emu is hairlike, not feathery. Emus defend themselves by kicking.

The Australian cassowary has a bony crest on its head. Like a rooster, it has red folds of skin that hang down through the neck. Cassowaries have rough and thick hair. They can grow up to six feet tall. They are bold fighters with long, sharp claws on their toes. They have even been known to kill people with their strong kicks.

The odd-looking New Zealand kiwi stands only a foot high. It weighs between 3 and 9 pounds. Its wings are so tiny that they are almost invisible. Kiwis have small heads, almost no neck, and very round bodies covered in coarse brown feathers. In truth, kiwis look sort of like hairy footballs!

8. What is the *main* idea of this passage?
   Ⓐ There are several kinds of unusual, flightless birds.
   Ⓑ Ostriches and emus are very similar in appearance.
   Ⓒ The kiwi is the strangest of all flightless birds.
   Ⓓ Birds that can't fly defend themselves by kicking.

9. Which detail supports the idea that the cassowary is a strange bird?
   Ⓐ It has plumage.
   Ⓑ It can run fast.
   Ⓒ It has claws.
   Ⓓ It has a bony crest on its head.

10. This passage suggests that
    Ⓐ ostriches are the prettiest of all birds.
    Ⓑ kiwis are the strangest looking birds.
    Ⓒ cassowaries are the least dangerous birds.
    Ⓓ emus are the most unusual birds.

11. The ostrich looks awkward because it
    Ⓐ is the largest living bird.
    Ⓒ has long legs and a long neck.
    Ⓑ grazes on the plains.
    Ⓓ can run 35 miles an hour.

12. From this passage, you can infer that the *most* dangerous bird is the
    Ⓐ emu.
    Ⓒ kiwi.
    Ⓑ ostrich.
    Ⓓ cassowary.

13. The purpose of this passage is to
    Ⓐ tell an entertaining story about birds.
    Ⓑ explain why some birds cannot fly.
    Ⓒ describe the animals of Australia.
    Ⓓ give information about birds.

14. Which sentence states an opinion?
    Ⓐ Kiwis look sort of like hairy footballs!
    Ⓑ The ostrich can run up to 35 miles an hour.
    Ⓒ Emus defend themselves by kicking.
    Ⓓ The ostrich is the largest living bird.

15. What is the *main* difference between emus and ostriches?
    Ⓐ their size
    Ⓑ their speed
    Ⓒ their awkward appearance
    Ⓓ their way of defending themselves

16. Which sentence states a fact?
    Ⓐ The ostrich has beautiful plumage.
    Ⓑ Emus weigh about 120 pounds.
    Ⓒ Kiwis look like hairy footballs.
    Ⓓ Cassowaries are bold birds.

Diagnostic Assessment

Comprehension

Read each passage and answer the questions that follow.

Quicksand

When you hear the word *quicksand*, what image comes to mind? You probably picture someone up to the waist in wet sand, screaming for help. In fact, quicksand can be very dangerous. People and animals have sunk into quicksand before and never escaped. However, the more you know about quicksand, the safer you will be.

First, quicksand is really just ordinary sand. It isn't some sort of strange hungry beast. Quicksand forms when water seeps up from underneath a layer of fine sand. The water pushes the grains of sand apart and makes the sand loose. This loose sand will not hold up a heavy weight.

Quicksand usually forms along the banks of rivers, at the seashore, or under slow-moving rivers and streams. It only forms when water flows upward through the sand, not over it. If you are in a place that tends to have quicksand, it's a good idea to carry a large stick. As you walk, poke the ground in front of you to be sure it's firm.

Let's suppose that you happen to step into some quicksand. The best way to deal with it is to stay calm. You may sink, but you won't sink quickly. You will have time to try several ways to get out. First, drop anything you might be carrying that adds weight, such as a backpack. Then try walking out—making slow and steady movements with your legs. If this doesn't work, the best thing to do is lie back and float. It's even easier to float on quicksand than on regular water.

Of course, you will want to call for help. If help is nearby, it's best simply to wait. If help is not nearby, then continue to lie on your back but make slow, rolling movements toward the edge of the quicksand. When you feel solid ground underneath, you can stand up.

Some animals seem to know how to avoid sinking down into quicksand. Mules, for instance, fold their legs underneath them and float on their bellies. Cows, on the other hand, tend to panic and wave their legs around. This doesn't help them escape. So, if you are ever trapped in quicksand, think like a mule, not like a cow.

Reading Comprehension Grades K-6

1. What is the *main* idea of this passage?
   Ⓐ Quicksand isn't really made up of sand.
   Ⓑ Quicksand can be dangerous, but there are ways to escape.
   Ⓒ You should poke the ground in front of you with a stick.
   Ⓓ Animals are able to float on quicksand, but humans always sink.

2. Which detail supports the idea that quicksand can be dangerous?
   Ⓐ Quicksand forms when water seeps up from underneath.
   Ⓑ You will have time to try several ways to get out.
   Ⓒ Animals have fallen into quicksand and never escaped.
   Ⓓ Quicksand is really just ordinary sand.

3. If you get caught in quicksand, what should you do first?
   Ⓐ Wave your arms and legs quickly.
   Ⓑ Drop anything heavy that you are carrying.
   Ⓒ Fold your legs underneath you.
   Ⓓ Poke a stick into the ground in front of you.

4. How is quicksand different from regular sand?
   Ⓐ It is darker.
   Ⓑ It is more dense.
   Ⓒ It is warmer.
   Ⓓ It is looser.

5. Which sentence states an opinion?

    Ⓐ Quicksand forms when water seeps up from underneath a layer of fine sand.

    Ⓑ People and animals have sunk into quicksand before and never escaped.

    Ⓒ Quicksand is a strange hungry beast.

    Ⓓ Quicksand forms along the banks of rivers, at the seashore, or under slow-moving rivers and streams.

6. The author's *main* purpose in this passage is to

    Ⓐ give information about quicksand.

    Ⓑ tell an entertaining story.

    Ⓒ persuade people to avoid quicksand.

    Ⓓ explain how quicksand forms.

7. Why should you drop anything heavy if you are stuck in quicksand?

    Ⓐ The heavy object in the sand might help push you out.

    Ⓑ Carrying more weight on your body will cause you to sink faster.

    Ⓒ You need your arms free to wave them in the air.

    Ⓓ The drop sound might be heard by someone who can help.

8. How is the mule's reaction to quicksand different from a cow's reaction?

    Ⓐ Mules fold their legs and float on their bellies.

    Ⓑ Mules wave their legs around.

    Ⓒ Mules sink immediately.

    Ⓓ Mules panic and splash their legs around.

The Train Track Mystery

"What's this?" wondered Jenna. She held up a piece of track from a child's train set. A gleam from the track had caught Jenna's eye as she waited in the city train station for her aunt and cousins to arrive.

"Jenna, over here!" cried Aunt Carrie. Jenna knew that her four cousins—Brenda, Kelly, Dawn, and Patsy—couldn't be far behind, so she stashed the piece of track in her backpack and headed toward her aunt. "I'll figure this one out later," thought Jenna.

That night, after finishing her homework and making sure her cousins were asleep, Jenna pulled out the piece of track and studied it. She concluded that it must have come from a very old toy train set, and she wondered how it ended up in the city station. Jenna fell asleep holding the piece of track. She dreamed that she was a girl living back in 1920, and although it had been a difficult year for the family, her parents had purchased a train set for her birthday. It was the circus train that she had wanted so badly after seeing it pictured in a catalog.

Jenna woke up early to the racket of her four-year-old cousin Patsy singing "I've Been Working on the Railroad" at the top of her lungs. "So have I," thought Jenna with a smile. She wanted to study the piece of track again and begin solving the mystery, but then she remembered that today was her great-grandfather's 90th birthday. The family was giving him a surprise party, and it was Jenna's job to find him a present. It had to be something he really wanted and didn't already have, but Jenna had spent a week on this task already and still didn't know what to get.

Suddenly, Jenna had an idea. She would find the owner of the toy train, buy the train, and surprise Great-Grandpa with it. Jenna knew that her great-grandfather liked riding on trains and probably had liked playing with them as a kid, too.

Jenna called every toy store and hobby shop she could find in the local phone book. No one had sold an old train set recently, but one woman suggested she call Depot Antiques. The man who answered the phone there said the track sounded like it had come from an old toy train set he had sold a week before to an older man—a Mr. Samuel Porter. Jenna thanked the man and said goodbye. Then she quickly looked up Mr. Porter in the phone book and called him.

Mr. Porter listened carefully to everything Jenna told him and was quite surprised. He had, in fact, bought the antique train set for his grandson, and one piece was missing when he got it home. Yes, he had passed through the city train station on his way home that day, and perhaps he had dropped the piece of track on the floor and not noticed. Would he sell Jenna the train? Yes, but only for one day. The price? A double birthday party for his grandson, Jeremy, and her great-grandfather. It seemed they had both been born on the same day—85 years apart!

When Mr. Porter and Jeremy arrived that afternoon, it was Jenna's turn to be surprised. Jeremy was just as Jenna had pictured him—an adorable and bright-eyed five-year-old. The surprise was that he was sitting in a wheelchair. Jenna introduced Mr. Porter and Jeremy to the rest of her family, and Mr. Porter said, "Please, call me Sam." Jeremy giggled and handed the train set to Jenna, and then everyone helped to put it together as they waited for Great-Grandpa to arrive.

Great-Grandpa was delighted with the party. He was so pleased to see all of his children, grandchildren, and great-grandchildren—all girls. He joked when he saw Jeremy that it was nice to have another male around. Then he spotted the train set, and his eyes lit up. "The Big Circus Train set! The one I wanted as a boy! How did you know? Where did you find it?"

Jenna explained how she'd found the piece of track and how it had led her to Jeremy and his grandfather. Great-Grandpa seemed to like the story almost as much as the train set. "I love a good mystery," he commented. "You would make an excellent detective, Jenna."

All afternoon, Jeremy sat right next to Great-Grandpa, and the two of them took turns making the sound of a train whistle. All the kids, big and small, took turns running the train. Jenna had indeed gotten Great-Grandpa something he didn't already have and really wanted—a chance to be a kid again and play with the train set of his dreams.

9. Which sentence states a fact?
    Ⓐ Great-Grandpa was delighted with the party.
    Ⓑ "You would make an excellent detective, Jenna."
    Ⓒ She concluded that it must have come from a very old set train set.
    Ⓓ Jeremy and her great-grandfather were born on the very same day—85 years apart.

10. What was Jenna's problem?
    Ⓐ She had to meet Jeremy.
    Ⓑ She needed to find a good birthday present for her great-grandfather.
    Ⓒ She could not find her answers.
    Ⓓ She got lost on her way to the train station.

11. What question was Jenna trying to answer?
    Ⓐ Who is Jeremy?
    Ⓑ Where is the train set that is missing a piece?
    Ⓒ Why did she dream about being a girl in 1920?
    Ⓓ When will Aunt Carrie and her cousins visit again?

12. Which of these events happened first?
    Ⓐ Jenna dreamed about a train set.
    Ⓑ Jenna did her homework.
    Ⓒ Jenna met her aunt at the train station.
    Ⓓ Jenna pulled out the piece of track.

13. Jenna woke up early in the morning because
    Ⓐ her cousin was singing.
    Ⓑ the phone rang.
    Ⓒ a train whistled.
    Ⓓ Great-Grandpa called her.

14. The author's *main* purpose in this passage is to
    Ⓐ show how the main character solves a mystery.
    Ⓑ share information about different train sets.
    Ⓒ tell about Jenna's special birthday party.
    Ⓓ share a story about how Great-Grandpa and Jeremy met.

15. Why do you think Jenna dreamed of living as a girl in the 1920s?
    Ⓐ She was thinking about her Great-Grandpa's life in 1920s.
    Ⓑ She fell asleep holding a piece of a very old train set.
    Ⓒ She had just read a book about the 1920s.
    Ⓓ She had just learned about the 1920s era in school.

16. Which word *best* describes Mr. Porter?
    Ⓐ kind
    Ⓑ nervous
    Ⓒ strict
    Ⓓ rude

Reading Comprehension Grades K–6

Answer Key

KINDERGARTEN

1. 1st picture
2. 2nd picture
3. 3rd picture
4. 1st picture
5. 1st picture
6. 2nd picture

GRADE 1

1. C	5. C
2. B	6. A
3. A	7. A
4. C	8. A

GRADE 2

1. D	6. C
2. A	7. A
3. D	8. B
4. A	9. B
5. B	10. D

GRADE 3

1. D	6. B
2. A	7. A
3. B	8. C
4. A	9. D
5. B	10. B

GRADE 4

1. C	9. C
2. A	10. D
3. D	11. B
4. C	12. C
5. A	13. A
6. B	14. D
7. C	15. C
8. B	16. D

GRADE 5

1. B	9. D
2. C	10. B
3. A	11. C
4. C	12. D
5. B	13. D
6. D	14. A
7. C	15. A
8. A	16. B

GRADE 6

1. B	9. D
2. C	10. B
3. B	11. B
4. D	12. C
5. C	13. A
6. A	14. A
7. B	15. B
8. A	16. A

Scoring Chart

The Scoring Chart is provided for your convenience in grading your students' work.

- Find the column that shows the total number of items on the test.
- Find the row that matches the number of items answered correctly.
- The intersection of the column and the row provides the percentage score.

NUMBER CORRECT	TOTAL NUMBER OF ITEMS										
	6	7	8	9	10	11	12	13	14	15	16
1	17	14	13	11	10	9	8	8	7	7	6
2	33	29	25	22	20	18	17	15	14	13	13
3	50	43	38	33	30	27	25	23	21	20	19
4	67	57	50	44	40	36	33	31	29	27	25
5	83	71	63	56	50	45	42	38	36	33	31
6	100	86	75	67	60	55	50	46	46	40	38
7		100	88	78	70	64	58	54	50	47	44
8			100	89	80	73	67	62	57	53	50
9				100	90	82	75	69	64	60	56
10					100	91	83	77	71	67	63
11						100	92	85	79	73	69
12							100	95	86	80	75
13								100	93	87	81
14									100	93	88
15										100	94
16											100

Metacomprehension Strategy Index Grades 4-6

▶ **WHAT** The *Metacomprehension Strategy Index* (developed by Schmitt, 1988, 1990) assesses students' independent use of strategies before, during, and after reading. Students read a series of questions about their reading behaviors. Questions cover broad areas such as predicting and verifying, previewing, purpose setting, self-questioning, drawing from background knowledge, summarizing, and using appropriate fix-up strategies.

Predicting and Verifying: Items numbered 1, 4, 13, 15, 16, 18, 23

Predicting the content of a story promotes active comprehension by giving readers a purpose for reading. Evaluating predictions and generating new ones as necessary enhances the constructive nature of the reading process.

Previewing: Items numbered 2, 3

Previewing the text facilitates comprehension by activating background knowledge and providing information for making predictions.

Purpose Setting: Items numbered 5, 7, 21

Reading with a purpose promotes active, strategic reading.

Self-Questioning: Items numbered 6, 14, 17

Generating questions to be answered promotes active comprehension by giving readers a purpose for reading.

Drawing from Background Knowledge: Items numbered 8, 9, 10, 19, 24, 25

Activating and incorporating information from background knowledge contributes to comprehension by helping readers make inferences and generate predictions.

Summarizing and Applying Fix-Up Strategies: Items numbered 11, 12, 20, 22

Summarizing the content at various points in the story serves as a form of comprehension monitoring. Rereading when comprehension breaks down represents strategic reading.
(from *Metacognition in Literacy Learning;* S. Israel, C. C. Block, K. Bauserman, K. Kinnucan-Welsch, 2005, page 105)

▶ **WHY** Comprehension is the ultimate goal of reading. Developing skilled, independent, strategic readers is the goal of comprehension instruction. This assessment helps you determine if students are using strategies before, during, and after reading and which ones they might be using. The assessment can provide insights into each student's strategic processing of text and affect the amount and types of strategy instruction you provide to students.

▶ **HOW** Make booklets for students by copying the series of questions. Distribute the booklets to the students.

Explain to students that this test will help you determine the strategies they use while reading so you can help them become more skilled and strategic readers. Make sure students are sitting in a comfortable setting with minimal distractions, and encourage them to do their best on the test.

In order to administer the test efficiently and make the directions understandable, you should be familiar with the directions and the test items before the test is given. During the administration, monitor students closely to make sure that each student is following the directions, is on the correct item, and is marking the test form correctly.

▶ **WHAT IT MEANS** This assessment can be scored using the Answer Key at the end of this section (page 305). It lists the correct response for each question. Mark each incorrect item on the student's test and record the number of correct items by category: Before Reading, During Reading, After Reading. In addition, use the item analysis information on pages 297–298 to determine which types of strategies students are not using (e.g., summarizing and fix-up strategies as indicated by items 11, 12, 20, and 22).

Use the results of the assessment to form small groups based on strategy needs. Provide additional instruction on these strategies during small-group time, and help students apply the strategies using the Skills-Based Practice Readers. In addition, reinforce those strategies not mastered during whole-group reading sessions in which students are asked to explain their self-selected strategy use.

Reading Comprehension Grades K-6

METACOMPREHENSION STRATEGY INDEX

Directions: Think about what kinds of things you can do to understand a story better before, during, and after you read it. Read each of the lists of four statements and decide which one of them would help *you* the most. *There are no right answers*. It is just what *you* think would help the most. Circle the letter of the statement you choose.

I. In each set of four, choose the one statement which tells a good thing to do to help you understand a story better *before* you read it.

1. Before I begin reading, it's a good idea to
   - Ⓐ see how many pages are in the story.
   - Ⓑ look up all of the big words in the dictionary.
   - Ⓒ make some guesses about what I think will happen in the story.
   - Ⓓ think about what has happened so far in the story.

2. Before I begin reading, it's a good idea to
   - Ⓐ look at the pictures to see what the story is about.
   - Ⓑ decide how long it will take me to read the story.
   - Ⓒ sound out the words I don't know.
   - Ⓓ check to see if the story is making sense.

3. Before I begin reading, it's a good idea to
   - Ⓐ ask someone to read the story to me.
   - Ⓑ read the title to see what the story is about.
   - Ⓒ check to see if most of the words have long or short vowels in them.
   - Ⓓ check to see if the pictures are in order and make sense.

4. Before I begin reading, it's a good idea to
   - Ⓐ check to see that no pages are missing.
   - Ⓑ make a list of words I'm not sure about.
   - Ⓒ use the title and pictures to help me make guesses about what will happen in the story.
   - Ⓓ read the last sentence so I will know how the story ends.

METACOMPREHENSION STRATEGY INDEX (continued)

5. Before I begin reading, it's a good idea to
   - Ⓐ decide on why I am going to read the story.
   - Ⓑ use the difficult words to help me make guesses about what will happen in the story.
   - Ⓒ reread some parts to see if I can figure out what is happening if things aren't making sense.
   - Ⓓ ask for help with the difficult words.

6. Before I begin reading, it's a good idea to
   - Ⓐ retell all of the main points that have happened so far.
   - Ⓑ ask myself questions that I would like to have answered in the story.
   - Ⓒ think about the meanings of the words which have more than one meaning.
   - Ⓓ look through the story to find all of the words with three or more syllables.

7. Before I begin reading, it's a good idea to
   - Ⓐ check to see if I have read this story before.
   - Ⓑ use my questions and guesses as a reason for reading the story.
   - Ⓒ make sure I can pronounce all of the words before I start.
   - Ⓓ think of a better title for the story.

8. Before I begin reading, it's a good idea to
   - Ⓐ think of what I already know about the things I see in the pictures.
   - Ⓑ see how many pages are in the story.
   - Ⓒ choose the best part of the story to read again.
   - Ⓓ read the story aloud to someone.

9. Before I begin reading, it's a good idea to
   - Ⓐ practice reading the story aloud.
   - Ⓑ retell all of the main points to make sure I can remember the story.
   - Ⓒ think of what the people in the story might be like.
   - Ⓓ decide if I have enough time to read the story.

METACOMPREHENSION STRATEGY INDEX (continued)

10. Before I begin reading, it's a good idea to
   - Ⓐ check to see if I am understanding the story so far.
   - Ⓑ check to see if the words have more than one meaning.
   - Ⓒ think about where the story might be taking place.
   - Ⓓ list all of the important details.

II. **In each set of four, choose the one statement which tells a good thing to do to help you understand a story better *while* you are reading it.**

11. While I'm reading, it's a good idea to
   - Ⓐ read the story very slowly so that I will not miss any important parts.
   - Ⓑ read the title to see what the story is about.
   - Ⓒ check to see if the pictures have anything missing.
   - Ⓓ check to see if the story is making sense by seeing if I can tell what's happened so far.

12. While I'm reading, it's a good idea to
   - Ⓐ stop to retell the main points to see if I am understanding what has happened so far.
   - Ⓑ read the story quickly so that I can find out what happened.
   - Ⓒ read only the beginning and the end of the story to find out what it is about.
   - Ⓓ skip the parts that are too difficult for me.

13. While I'm reading, it's a good idea to
   - Ⓐ look all of the big words up in the dictionary.
   - Ⓑ put the book away and find another one if things aren't making sense.
   - Ⓒ keep thinking about the title and the pictures to help me decide what is going to happen next.
   - Ⓓ keep track of how many pages I have left to read.

METACOMPREHENSION STRATEGY INDEX (continued)

14. While I'm reading, it's a good idea to
    - Ⓐ keep track of how long it is taking me to read the story.
    - Ⓑ check to see if I can answer any of the questions I asked before I started reading.
    - Ⓒ read the title to see what the story is going to be about.
    - Ⓓ add the missing details to the pictures.

15. While I'm reading, it's a good idea to
    - Ⓐ have someone read the story aloud to me.
    - Ⓑ keep track of how many pages I have read.
    - Ⓒ list the story's main character.
    - Ⓓ check to see if my guesses are right or wrong.

16. While I'm reading, it's a good idea to
    - Ⓐ check to see that the characters are real.
    - Ⓑ make a lot of guesses about what is going to happen next.
    - Ⓒ not look at the pictures because they might confuse me.
    - Ⓓ read the story aloud to someone.

17. While I'm reading, it's a good idea to
    - Ⓐ try to answer the questions I asked myself.
    - Ⓑ try not to confuse what I already know with what I'm reading about.
    - Ⓒ read the story silently.
    - Ⓓ check to see if I am saying the new vocabulary words correctly.

18. While I'm reading, it's a good idea to
    - Ⓐ try to see if my guesses are going to be right or wrong.
    - Ⓑ reread to be sure I haven't missed any of the words.
    - Ⓒ decide on why I am reading the story.
    - Ⓓ list what happened first, second, third, and so on.

METACOMPREHENSION STRATEGY INDEX (continued)

19. While I'm reading, it's a good idea to
    Ⓐ see if I can recognize the new vocabulary words.
    Ⓑ be careful not to skip any parts of the story.
    Ⓒ check to see how many of the words I already know.
    Ⓓ keep thinking of what I already know about the things and ideas in the story to help me decide what is going to happen.

20. While I'm reading, it's a good idea to
    Ⓐ reread some parts or read ahead to see if I can figure out what is happening if things aren't making sense.
    Ⓑ take my time reading so that I can be sure I understand what is happening.
    Ⓒ change the ending so that it makes sense.
    Ⓓ check to see if there are enough pictures to help make the story ideas clear.

III. In each set of four, choose the one statement which tells a good thing to do to help you understand a story better *after* you have read it.

21. After I've read a story, it's a good idea to
    Ⓐ count how many pages I read with no mistakes.
    Ⓑ check to see if there were enough pictures to go with the story to make it interesting.
    Ⓒ check to see if I met my purpose for reading the story.
    Ⓓ underline the causes and effects.

22. After I've read a story, it's a good idea to
    Ⓐ underline the main idea.
    Ⓑ retell the main points of the whole story so that I can check to see if I understood it.
    Ⓒ read the story again to be sure I said all of the words right.
    Ⓓ practice reading the story aloud.

METACOMPREHENSION STRATEGY INDEX (continued)

23. After I've read a story, it's a good idea to
    - Ⓐ read the title and look over the story to see what it is about.
    - Ⓑ check to see if I skipped any of the vocabulary words.
    - Ⓒ think about what made me make good or bad predictions.
    - Ⓓ make a guess about what will happen next in the story.

24. After I've read a story, it's a good idea to
    - Ⓐ look up all of the big words in the dictionary.
    - Ⓑ read the best parts aloud.
    - Ⓒ have someone read the story aloud to me.
    - Ⓓ think about how the story was like things I already knew about before I started reading.

25. After I've read a story, it's a good idea to
    - Ⓐ think about how I would have acted if I were the main character in the story.
    - Ⓑ practice reading the story silently for practice of good reading.
    - Ⓒ look over the story title and pictures to see what will happen.
    - Ⓓ make a list of the things I understood the most.

METACOMPREHENSION STRATEGY INDEX (continued)

DIRECTIONS FOR SCORING

Part One: Responses that indicate metacomprehension strategy awareness.

I. Before Reading:	II. During Reading:	III. After Reading:
1. C	11. D	21. C
2. A	12. A	22. B
3. B	13. C	23. C
4. C	14. B	24. D
5. A	15. D	25. A
6. B	16. B	
7. B	17. A	
8. A	18. A	
9. C	19. D	
10. C	20. A	

McLeod Assessment of Reading Comprehension

▶ **WHAT** The *McLeod Assessment of Reading Comprehension* assesses reading comprehension by means of the "cloze" technique, in which students read a series of passages and supply words that have been deleted from sentences within each passage. Supplying the correct word requires comprehension of the sentences within the passage. While the passages are ordered in respect to difficulty, individual passages do not represent a specific grade level like those that appear in the *Fry Oral Reading Test*. Interpretation is based on the total number of correct words supplied for all passages administered. Two levels of the test assess reading comprehension in grades 2–5 and in grades 6 and above.

▶ **WHY** Comprehension is the ultimate goal of reading. This assessment requires students to accurately decode words, to apply their knowledge of grammar, syntax, and vocabulary, and to use critical reading strategies that aid in the literal and inferential comprehension of what is read. When administered to everyone in a class, the *McLeod Assessment of Reading Comprehension* serves as a valuable screening tool for identifying students who may have reading difficulties and who may benefit from additional assessment that focuses on specific skills underlying reading. It is useful to test frequently in the elementary and middle school grades.

▶ **HOW** Make booklets for students by copying either the elementary or upper level test pages that follow. For the youngest students, you may want to use only the first two to four passages of the elementary level. Distribute the booklets to the students.

Reading Comprehension Grades K–6

SAY: *Do not open your booklets. There are some silent reading puzzles in these booklets. Some words are missing from sentences, and you have to write in the word that you think should go in each blank space. Let's do the first sample together.*

Work through the example paragraph aloud with the students. Read the first sentence, pausing for the blank, and have the students suggest an answer. Have them write the answer in the proper space. Repeat this process with the second sentence. Then have the students read the third sentence to themselves and fill in the answer. Check their work.

SAY: *In the paragraphs inside the booklet, write the one word in each blank that you think should go there. Just write one word in each blank space. If you can't think of a word, go on to the next one. When you come to the end of the first page, go straight to the second without waiting to be told, and continue until you come to the end.*

You have 15 minutes to complete the test. If you do finish before the time is up, look over your work. Don't worry about the correct spelling—this is not a spelling test. Try to spell each word as best you can.

After answering any questions, have students begin. After the time has expired or when students appear to have finished, ask students to stop.

This is not a strictly timed test. Students should be given a reasonable amount of time to complete the test. You may want to adjust the time limit if you are giving students fewer passages to complete.

▶ **WHAT IT MEANS** Use the scoring key that follows each form to correct the students' work. Place the total number of words correctly scored in the box after each passage. Then determine the total score and enter it on page 1 of the test booklet. Refer to the scoring criteria on the following page to determine approximate reading grade level. For those students whose reading comprehension is below their current grade level, additional assessments should be administered that evaluate specific reading comprehension skills.

Diagnostic Assessment

Reading Comprehension Grades K-6

Scoring Criteria **Elementary Level**

Score	Reading Grade Level
1–4	Grade 1 and below
5–8	Grade 2, Early
9–14	Grade 2, Late
15–20	Grade 3, Early
21–25	Grade 3, Late
26–30	Grade 4, Early
31–34	Grade 4, Late
35–38	Grade 5, Early
39–42	Grade 5, Late
43–46	Grade 6, Early
47–49	Grade 6, Late
50–56	Grade 7 and above

Scoring Criteria **Upper Level**

Score	Reading Grade Level
1–40	Administer Elementary Level
41–55	Grade 7 and above

▶ **WHAT'S NEXT?** Students who score below grade level will benefit from an assessment provided by the *Fry Oral Reading Test,* the *San Diego Quick Assessment of Reading Ability,* and the *Critchlow Verbal Language Scales* to determine if fluency, word recognition, or vocabulary deficits are the underlying causes of poor comprehension.

McLeod Assessment of Reading Comprehension, Elementary Level

Name_____ Grade_____ Date_____

DO NOT TURN OVER THE PAGE UNTIL YOU ARE TOLD.

Pat Has a Cold

Pat did _____ feel very well. Dad

gave her _____ hot milk. She drank the

milk and went to rest _____ her bed.

TOTAL SCORE

Diagnostic Assessment

A Hungry Cat

Kitty jumped up and sat on the table. She watched the fish swim

round _____ round in the glass bowl. She tried

_____ push the bowl with _____ paw,

but could not tip _____ over.

A Trip to the Hospital

Mike woke up in the middle of the night _____

called out for his mother and father. He _____ them that

he was _____ feeling well and that _____

was a sharp pain _____ his side. Wrapping him

_____ a blanket, Mike's parents rushed _____

to the hospital. A _____ examined him and informed

his _____ that an operation was necessary.

GO TO THE NEXT PAGE.

Scottie Raises the Alarm

Something seemed to be wrong with Scottie, the family dog, when

she woke up suddenly late one winter evening. _____

air was filled with smoke, and flames _____ coming

from the stove in the corner _____ the kitchen.

She ran upstairs to where the family was sleeping and began

_____ bark loudly. Suddenly, the lights were

switched _____ in each bedroom and Scottie

watched _____ waited until the family

_____ gone downstairs. Then she followed them

_____ of the house and into _____

cool night air.

A Modern Pirate

Carol had just finished reading a book about the pirates who used

_____ sail the seven seas. She closed _____

eyes and soon she was asleep and dreaming _____ she

was a pirate. She was not like the pirate in the book but one who flew

_____ spaceship and attacked other spaceships. Instead

_____ gold, silver, and diamonds, her booty included

precious fuels _____ expensive computers.

GO TO THE NEXT PAGE.

Diagnostic Assessment

Joshua

Each day Joshua woke at six in the morning. For most boys of

his age, _____ to school was only a dream. Joshua

himself had to _____ to provide money for the

members _____ his family. Each day he had an hour's walk

_____ the capital city where _____

would pick up a box containing plastic jewelry. For _____

next ten hours he _____ walk the streets, stopping

tourists and begging them to buy some of the jewelry. The only

_____ he rested was during the hottest part of the

_____, when he was able to drink _____

tepid water and to _____ the orange that he had

picked up at the market. At the _____ of the day he would

receive the few coins that made up his pay, walk _____,

eat a small supper, and then _____ asleep. He was always

_____ tired to enjoy the normal life of a young boy.

GO TO THE NEXT PAGE.

In the Valley of the Unknown Planet

Listen. Can you hear that whistling noise? It seems to be

_____ from that mountain. Kris and Michael volunteered

to _____ out and investigate. They put on their

_____ suits and grabbed their laser pistols. They

_____ the safety of their underground headquarters and

began _____ cross the empty terrain that lay before

_____. Without encountering any problems

they reached _____ mountain. Their bulky space

suits _____ climbing difficult but after a few

hours _____ reached the summit of the _____.

Before them stood a huge monument that _____ been

constructed by previous settlers. The whistling started _____

and now the two spacemen _____ the cause.

STOP. LOOK OVER YOUR WORK UNTIL TIME IS UP.

Scoring Key – Elementary Level

Correct responses for each passage are listed below. Mark errors in the test booklet. Do not count misspellings as an error. Count the number of correct responses and record this number in the space provided on the first page of the test booklet.

Pat Has a Cold

n't; not
some
in; on

A Hungry Cat

and
to
her
it

A Trip to the Hospital

and
told
not; n't
there
in
in
him
doctor
parents

Scottie Raises the Alarm

The; the
were
of
to
on
and
had
out
the

A Modern Pirate

to
her
that
a
of
and

Joshua

going
work
of
to
he
the

Joshua (continued)

would
time
day
some
eat
end
home
fall
too

In the Valley of the Unknown Planet

coming
go
space
left
to
them
the
made
they
mountain
had
again
knew

McLeod Assessment of Reading Comprehension, Upper Level

Name_____ Grade_____ Date_____

DO NOT TURN OVER THE PAGE UNTIL YOU ARE TOLD.

Pat Has a Cold

Pat did _____ feel very well. Dad

gave her _____ hot milk. She drank the

milk and went to rest _____ her bed.

TOTAL SCORE

Diagnostic Assessment

Mrs. Hill and Her Garden

Everyone on West Street knows Mrs. Hill.

_____ is the little old lady who lives _____ the little white house.

All summer long _____ is out working in her garden. This _____ is what she likes to do best _____ all.

"Hello, Mrs. Hill," her friends say _____ they go by. "May we help you?"

Mrs. _____ always says with a smile, "No, _____ you." And she goes on working with _____ many plants and flowers.

One day last month, Mrs. Hill looked around _____ garden. She looked _____ at the sky. "It is _____ to take my house plants in," she _____ "It will start to get cold soon."

_____ by one, Mrs. Hill took her plants _____ the house.

GO TO THE NEXT PAGE.

The Enemy

In a corner of Mrs. Smith's living _____ hangs a golden cage. The cage is _____ home of Goldie, the parrot. Mrs. Smith also _____ a very haughty cat who, come what may, _____ be the master of the _____.

For several days now the cat has noticed _____ Mrs. Smith has been paying more _____ to Goldie. She never stops saying: "What _____ darling he is! How sweet he is! _____ well he talks!"

The cat is fed _____. He notices that it is easy for _____ mistress to open the cage to feed _____ bird. So he takes advantage of her absence and, by _____ the cage door with _____ paw, lets the bird escape.

GO TO THE NEXT PAGE.

The Clever Crow

A thirsty crow found a water jug. Since there _____

only a little water in _____, she could not reach it

with her _____. She hopped back a few steps and

_____ flew against the jug. The jug did _____

move from its place. The crow saw _____ it was too

heavy. But now she brought little stones _____ the field and

threw _____ into the jug, so that the _____

soon rose higher. At last she could dip _____ beak into the

water and quench her _____.

GO TO THE NEXT PAGE.

Once Upon a Time

Once upon a time there was a prisoner whom nobody ever

_____ to see, and to whom no friend ever came to say

_____ kind word in his dark _____. He led a

dreary, wretched life, but one _____ a little mouse came out

of a _____ in the corner. As it was _____ timid, it

disappeared as soon as the _____ moved, but soon it came

back. _____ threw it a crumb from his scanty meal. From

then on the little mouse _____ back to see him every day.

It _____ to come and snuggle up against his

neck or play on _____ hands. To cut a long story

_____, they became real friends, and his dark

_____ never seemed as lonesome _____

the prisoner when the little mouse _____ there.

STOP. LOOK OVER YOUR WORK UNTIL TIME IS UP.

Reading Comprehension Grades K–6

Scoring Key – Upper Level

Correct responses for each passage are listed below. Mark errors in the test booklet. Do not count misspellings as an error. Count the number of correct responses and record this number in the space provided on the first page of the test booklet.

Pat Has a Cold

n't; not
some
in; on

Mrs. Hill and Her Garden

she
in
she
work
of
as
Hill
thank
her
at
up
time
said
One
into

The Enemy

room
the
has
will
house
that
attention
a
How
up
his/the
the
opening
his

The Clever Crow

was
it
beak
then
not
that

The Clever Crow
(continued)

from
them
water
her
thirst

Once Upon a Time

came
a
cell
day
hole
very
prisoner
He
came
used
his
short
cell
to
was

Teacher Notes

Teacher Notes

Teacher Notes

Teacher Notes

Teacher Notes

Teacher Notes

Teacher Notes

Teacher Notes

Teacher Notes

Teacher Notes